WYSIWYG Tales

Bill Flury

ISBN-13: 978-1494256975
ISBN-10: 1494256975
CreateSpace Independent Publishing Platform; 2 edition

DEDICATION

To Mary

WYSIWYG TALES

Foreword

You can call me the WYSIWYG Wizard. My Wizard license permits me to help you, your colleagues, and your friends find ways to see, better understand, and improve the things you do and the ways you do them.

In The Wizard of Oz movie, Dorothy and her companions had, within themselves, the traits they sought but could not see. The Wizard found ways to help them see those things. There was no real magic in what he did. He just created situations in which their actions made it easy for them to visualize the fact that those traits had always been there. All he did was help them see.

That's the kind of thing I do. The people I work with do many different types of things. They build things, they write things, and they change things. Sometimes they work alone and sometimes they work with other people to provide services or complete projects. And, like the seekers in the movie, they cannot always see clearly what they do. They do well most of the time but they also have problems, make mistakes, and have crises. They would very much like to avoid all of those difficulties but they can't see how to do that. You, your friends, and your co-workers may be like that also. You may be skipping down your own yellow brick road, doing what you do, not fully seeing and understanding what you do and how you fit in all that.

A little bit of WYSIWYG wizardry can help you see how to do all those things. No magic is required. All you need are some simple, down-to-earth, practical visualization techniques to help you see, better understand, and improve what you do and the way you do it.

Take a moment and ask yourself how well you can:

- See and understand how things you do fit together – or not
- See ways to solve your problems and avoid crises
- See how you can improve coordination with colleagues and friends
- Help others see beneficial things they can or should be doing
- See how to organize your thoughts and activities
- See things that are really important and focus attention on them

Here, in ***WYSIWYG Tales***, you will find tales about people I have worked with who have found various ways to get a clear picture and full understanding of the things they are doing and how these have helped them. I hope you will find in these tales some ideas about useful ways to see what you do that will help you.

Follow me into the rest of the book. Read the tales and learn how you can see things about what you do that you have never been able to see before. See and learn some practical visualization techniques that you and the others on the road with you will be able to use to be more successful.

What You See Is What You Get

WYSIWYG

CONTENTS

INTRODUCTION

It's really pretty amazing! You are at your computer, writing a report, designing a graphic or calculating with a spreadsheet and you can almost instantly see the results of your inputs unfold before your eyes. That's the wizardry of programs that record and show you exactly what you are thinking and doing. It has taken over 60 years and untold amounts of programmer time to achieve this. Now, when you work at a computer What You See Is What You Get and we call that WYSIWYG.

It's wonderful to have almost instant feedback as you think and work. But, there's Good News and Bad News about that. The Good News about WYSIWYG is that you can work like a sculptor. You can instantly see all the wonderful things in your head come out to where you can see them.

The Bad News is that WYSIWYG is completely impartial. While you can see and appreciate the good things, you can also almost instantly see all the flaws. But, as you think about it, that's really a good thing because, when you can see the flaws you can figure out how to fix them.

What WYSIWYG Helps You See

Let's start with the easy things, the typos and grammatical errors. Somehow or other, what has been in your head hasn't made the trip through your fingers to the keyboard, mouse or stylus error free. There are plenty of apps to take care of those flaws. So, let's not worry about those. Some other flaws are harder to deal with. These are the flaws related to the things you know and remember – or don't -- and the way you are thinking.

Information Flaws

When what you are thinking about is only in your head it's hard for you to see what those thoughts are and be able to clear them up. You have distractions, you can forget things. You may even have some misconceptions about some things.

As you work you may see that you have not included some information that is important to your argument or story. This may be information that you know but just forgot or may be information or data you still need to collect. It can also be information that you have but, for some reason or other, may have ignored. Actually seeing the information gaps on the screen or on a printout makes them real and gives you something tangible that you can work on to fix.

As former Secretary of Defense Don Rumsfeld noted, ***"There are things we know that we know. ... there are things that we know we don't know ... but there are also things we don't know we don't know".*** You may not see what you need to know until your personal version of WYSIWYG brings it out for you to see.

Logic Flaws

WYSIWYG lets you see if what you are thinking needs work. When you see what you are creating you may discover that the logic or sequence of your presentation just doesn't hold up. You may have been sure that what you had in your mind would work but when you can actually see it on the screen or print it out it just doesn't seem to work.

WYSIWYG Without a Computer

Some people have what might be called "In-Head WYSIWYG". The genius theoretical physicists at the Institute for Advanced Study, where Albert Einstein once worked, play chess in their faculty lounge for relaxation. There are no pieces on their chess board. They don't need to see them. As a player's turn comes up he just announces his move to his opponent. They see what they are getting without having to show it on the board. They would only need to have the pieces there to show others how the match is progressing.

Those of us who are not genius physicists need to have good WYSIWYG tools to see what we are thinking. We all have different preferred ways to see and there are many ways to translate what we are thinking into tangible form.

Daniel Boorstin, an historian and educator, expresses very well how the WYSIWYG concept worked for him. He worked with paper and pencil (i.e., early WYSIWYG) and he said: ***"I write to discover what I think".*** He would write, then read what he wrote, see if that was what he was really thinking, and then re-write until he got his facts and his thinking straight.

You don't need a computer to make the WYSIWYG concept work for you. Boorstin used paper and pencil. This Wizard uses a whiteboard and markers or, sometimes, a blank wall with sticky notes to see and share with others what he is getting. Artists use paints on canvas, chefs use recipes, composers use sheet music, and perfume makers prepare samples. Whatever works.

You can develop your own WYSIWYG environment. In the tales that follow you will see a variety of different ways that people have found to see what they are getting – their own personal WYSIWYG so to speak. Perhaps their tales will help you:

- See ways to solve your problems
- See how to better organize your thoughts and activities
- See things that are really important in what you are doing
- See and understand how things you do really work and can be made to work better
- See and improve coordination within your team and with others
- Help others see things they could or should be doing

What Comes Next

There are many WYSIWYG tales to tell. We will begin with the tale of Sarah and how she found a WYSIWYG way to see and resolve her problem. But, before we start, you need to know that Sarah's tale and all the others to follow are true tales about real people who have worked with this Wizard at one time or another throughout his long career in process improvement.

As you read about Sarah, Fred, Anne, Ernie, and all the others in the various stories, see if you can find similarities to your situation and the things you would really like to be able to see better. When you can develop your own WYSIWYG ways you will be able to see how to be better at what you do and how to avoid the errors, misunderstandings, crises and all the other things that steal joy from your life.

Let's move on to Sarah's tale. She is a publications coordinator. She works with engineers and graphics artists. She's been getting a lot of complaints from both groups and she can't see why. Wait until you see the problem she had and how she resolved it.

You may have a problem like hers and can do what she did to solve it.

A coordinator is a person with a desk between two expediters.

-- Anon

SARAH'S TALE

Sarah Has a Problem

Sarah was having a bad day, one of many in the past few weeks. Things just weren't working as she expected them to. She was doing what she had been doing all along but, for some reason, some things were not going right. She couldn't see what was happening. She asked me if there was some way I could help her see what was causing the problems.

Sarah worked in a high-tech organization that was staffed by a lot of engineers and programmers. They did analyses, conducted studies, and developed designs and produced reports about those things for their clients. Sarah's job was to take the draft reports produced by the staff, get them paired with the appropriate graphics, get them to conform to the company formatting standards, and prepare them for final printing and delivery.

At our first meeting, I asked Sarah to show me in detail what she did so we could walk through the process and discuss it. Sarah gave me a quick overview of what she did. She mentioned that in the last few weeks some of the engineers had told her that they were upset about the graphics being produced for their reports. They felt that charts being produced by the graphics staff were not accurately reflecting the story in the data. On the other hand, the graphics staff were complaining that the engineers weren't providing enough background information about the data. Sarah said that she was getting caught in the middle of the arguments as she tried to get everything pulled together for publication.

It's All In My Head

It sounded like there was some flaw in the process that was causing these problems and we should try to find that flaw and fix it. So, I asked Sarah, "Do you have a written description of what you do?" Sarah said, "No". "Do you have notes that you took when you were being shown or told what to do?" Sarah said, "No". "Do you have a checklist or a set of instructions, or a manual that you follow? Sarah said, "No". She finally said, "It's just all in my head".

We agreed that just having it all in her head was not very good. We couldn't use that to find and fix any flaws in the process. There were several problems. First, what she was seeing In her head was obviously not clear enough to enable her to see what was causing her frequent problems. Second, we discussed the fact that what she was seeing in her head, her Mind's Eye" so-to-speak, was an imperfect picture. She might be missing some of the details or remembering some things wrong. Finally, I told her I had to be able to see it also so we could work together to get what was causing her problems.

Seeing What's In Sarah's Head

As we started, I told her about something said by Bernard DeVoto, a great editor: ***"The best thing about writing something down is that then you can change it".***

Then, I said, "Trying to work with something you can't see (because it's not written down) is like trying to make a suit of clothes for a ghost. It won't work. So, we will have to work together to get it written down. Then we can find out what's not working and change it. So, go ahead and "wing it" – explain to me, from memory, what you do and we'll record it on the chalkboard".

Sarah started talking and I started drawing what she said as a process flow chart on the chalkboard. In the first pass, Sarah talked though everything she was doing and I kept drawing and writing notes as she talked. When Sarah got to the end, we both took a short break and then came back to look at the result.

Then, we walked through the flow chart again. Sarah saw things she had missed and some things that had not been correctly recorded. We fixed the chart so it accurately represented all that Sarah told me.

Then, I asked a Sarah a few questions.

- Are there some things you do without thinking?
- Are there some things you only do in certain circumstances?
- Do you have any checklists, "Sticky Notes" or other kinds of notes or reminders about any parts of this process?
- Are there any things in this picture that you think you do but, really, never do?

Those triggered Sarah's memory and we made a few additions and changes to the picture. Then, we wrote "SAVE" on the chalkboard and went home for the night.

The Next Day

The next day we asked two of the engineers who were frequent authors to come and walk through the chart with us. They clarified a few points and changed one task that involved checking for documentation standards that involved two steps instead of the one shown. Later in the day we did the same with two of the graphics staff members and had similar results.

Then We Began To See

The following day, we walked through the chart together. One thing became very clear. All the communication between the authors and the graphics people went through Sarah. There were no places in the flow chart where those two groups ever talked directly with each other. All of the products from each group passed Sarah on the way to the other. Likewise, and here was a key point, all of the complaints and problems also went through Sarah and she, as a coordinator did not have the authority to provide technical direction to either group.

Sarah thought about that for a moment and then commented. She said that it seemed unfair that she was being caught up in the arguments between the two groups. She said, "I think I see the problem. The problems we are having are their problems, not mine, and I should not be in the middle".

She looked back at the chart and said, "You know, if we added a task for the authors and the graphics people to get together while their documents are being drafted ..."

Wizard Comment

Creating the flow chart was, literally, an eye-opener for Sarah. When the things she was doing were only "in her head" they were floating about and were invisible to her and not really useful. As we drew the chart, Sarah was reminded of things that she and her co-workers did in the process without thinking. She also saw gaps in the process where there were things she did not know.

The sequencing of actions was not really as clear as it was later when the picture was up on the chalkboard. The problem was hiding in the details and Sarah had to bring out the details, make them visible, and stabilize them so she could see and get what was going on.

When she was done, for the first time, Sarah could clearly see how the whole process worked and how she and the others fit into it. She got a more complete understanding of what she needed to do to make the process work better.

What she saw, she got. Going back to the Wizard of Oz analogy – Sarah needed help to recall, describe, and define the details of her process and the relationships among the players. Once the process was written down on the chalkboard, as Bernard DeVoto told us, **she could change it, and she did.**

WYSIWYG

DIFFERENT WAYS TO SEE

"Seeing" In the Tales to Come

In Sarah's tale you saw someone who found a way to see what she was doing and get an understanding of how she could make it work better for herself and the others involved.

In the coming sections you will see tales about other people who found different ways to see what they were doing and get an understanding of how they could make it work better for them. You will see how two workgroups learned how to see their process flaws and fix them. You will see how Anne was able to see where she had spare moments in her work day and get ideas on how to make better use of them. You will see how Fred was finally able to see why he was always missing his deadlines and got a way to share his scheduling problems with the people who were causing it.

And so it will be with all the other tales. In each of these, you will see how the WYSIWYG approach helped bring out into the open and document the situation in a way that the players, their colleagues, and friends, could all see and share the same understanding of what they are seeing.

Different Way To See

As you read the tales to come it will become apparent to you that there are many differences in the way we see. The differences arise from two primary sources: 1) what our senses tell us, and; 2) the way we interpret that information based on our life experiences.

If we want to help our colleagues and friends see things the way we do we have to recognize the fact that everyone sees everything a bit differently. When you and someone else are looking at the same thing, you each see something different.

What do your senses and your experience tell you about the accompanying picture? Is this an argument over something – or is it a neighbor handing another neighbor a glass of lemonade on a hot day? What you see is what you get. **[The correct interpretation is the latter one.]**

Everyone Senses Differently

Suppose you are giving a presentation to a group of people about a wonderful new application you have developed for their cell phones. Some may have a color vision deficiency and will see all of your color charts and illustrations in shades of gray. Some may have a hearing deficiency and not hear the "beep" tone that is a key signal for the app. Some may not be able to sense the vibration that you use to provide a different signal. Ideally, the app does not include features that require taste or smell sensitivity. The question for you is, "Did everyone see what you were trying to have them get?" Not likely.

Everyone Interprets Differently

A nature photographer explained to the Wizard how your background shapes what you see. Early in her life she collected and arranged displays of insects then went on to study art, draw, paint, and eventually curate art exhibits. In retirement, she and her husband care for a wildlife preserve. She says that her paintings, sculpture, drawings, prints, and contacts with nature have all influenced the way she sees.

If you look at one of her flower photos you will see a nice photo of a flower. However, if you talk with her about the picture you will see much more. You will see how she was able to capture the environment, the history and the richness of the texture and color in the petals and leaves. In short, you will see all of what she sees and the way she sees it. What you see – with her help – is what you get.

WYSIWYG Can Be Personal

Some people can look at a spreadsheet full of data and "**See**" the story in the numbers. Others, whether they have math fright or some other aversion to numbers, may freeze up at a set of numbers and have to find a different way to see what is significant in the numbers.

Darrell Huff, in *How to Lie With Statistics*, says, "There is terror in numbers". Gerald Jones, in *How to Lie With Charts, says* "All charts distort the truth..." Mark Mononier in *How to Lie with Maps*, says about maps, "Despite their immense value, maps lie. In fact, they must".

To facilitate **seeing**, you must be aware of the possibilities for intentional or unintentional "lying" and the individual differences in the way people see. What works for some may not work for others. Be prepared to offer a variety of approaches. The Wizard's motto is "Use Whatever Works".

How the Secretary of Defense Preferred to See

Robert McNamara was Secretary of Defense during part of the Vietnam War. In his earlier work at Ford Motor Company he was the Chief Financial Officer for the company. He was very comfortable with numbers and spreadsheets. He based his decisions on what he saw in them. He was famous in the Defense Department for not allowing any data to be presented to him in the form of pie or bar charts or any other graphic representation. In his view, pictures could lie – only numbers could provide the true story.

Secretary McNamara's predilection for numbers was not unusual. Many people who are comfortable with numbers are like that. However, there are some who can only see the story in the numbers when they are presented as charts or graphs. That's the way it was for Ernie and Me.

Ernie and the Wizard

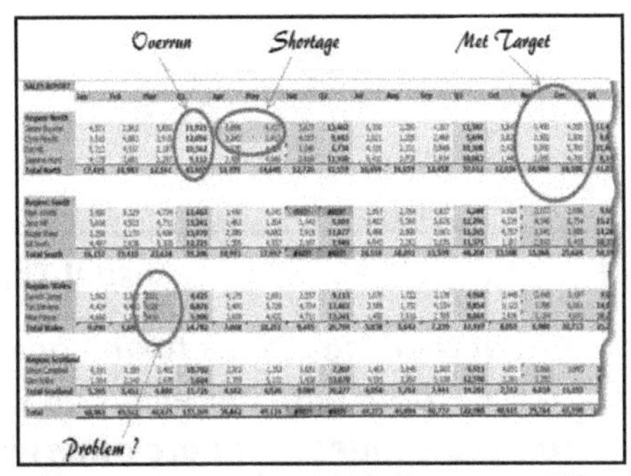

The Wizard's boss, Ernie was a retired Army general whose last post was as Comptroller of the Army. In that job he worked with lots of budget and expenditure data. Ernie could look at a spreadsheet filled with numbers and instantly "**See**" what the numbers were saying (e.g., Project X is overspent by 12%, Program Y is behind schedule and needs more funds). Ernie could "read" the numbers like others read words. Ernie brought that skill with him when he came to our company. He looked at the spreadsheets for our project data and spotted problems and trends instantly.

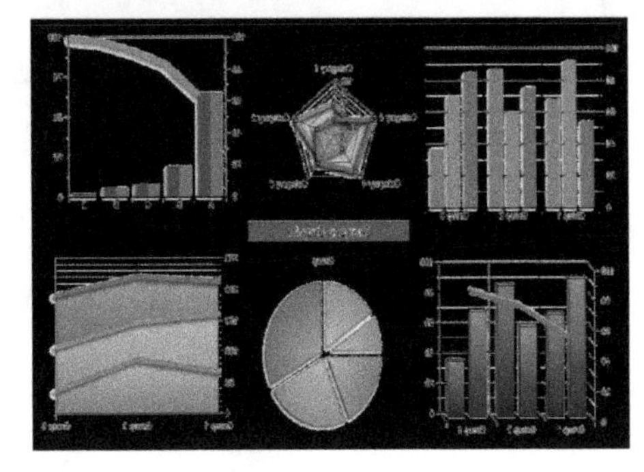

As Ernie's deputy, I also had to stay in touch with what was going on in the projects. My background was in language, devoid of numbers and filled with words and pictures. I could not do what Ernie did with numbers. I had to ask for the numbers to be presented as pie and bar charts and dashboard gauges so I could see what was going on. That worked for me. My way did not work very well for Ernie. So we agreed that we would each look at the data in our own way and would compare notes as we went along. That worked. We came to the same conclusions but each of us got there in our own way.

No Magic Required

There is no magic formula you can to use to make sure that everyone will see what you see the way that you see it. You need to be constantly aware of the existence of personal differences and be prepared to adjust to them. It's important! So, find and use whatever works.

As you read, look for the different ways the players found to see what they were doing and take advantage of their new insights. In the following sections tales are grouped by their similarities.

Visual Thinking

Visual thinking means taking advantage of our innate ability to see – both with our eyes and with our mind's eye – in order to discover ideas that are otherwise invisible, develop those ideas quickly and intuitively, and then share those ideas with other people in a way that they simply "get".

Dan Roam in *The Back of the Napkin*

WYSIWYG

Wizard's Tales Start Here

SEE HOW TO MAKE THINGS WORK BETTER

SEE HOW WE STOPPED BEING LATE

SEE HOW WE STOPPED MAKING MISTAKES

Good, Better, Best

Never let it rest

'til the Good is Better,

and the Better, Best

Mom

SEE HOW TO MAKE THINGS WORK BETTER

Two Groups With Problems

We'll start with tales about two work groups that had problems and could not see any way to fix them.

The first tale is about a group of four teams that kept missing deadlines because they never took time to see how their individual schedules affected the overall delivery schedule.

The second tale is about a programming group that was in trouble because its government client was rejecting too many of its products for having too many coding defects. These people were all supposed to be following a standard process for doing their work but everyone's view of the process was different enough to cause problems.

If you were the manager of either of these groups you would have been delighted by the extensive experience and expertise of all of their members. However, you would have been just as puzzled as they were by the problems they were having.

Because they were all deeply involved in what they were doing, each person had a clear picture in his head of what he or his group was doing – one piece of the puzzle, so to speak. Unfortunately, no one ever collected all the pieces and put them together

How They Managed To See

Ultimately, each group found its own way to collect all the pieces and put them together so that they could all see the whole process – the Big Picture – of what they were doing. At that point, they could see the reason for their problems and they could understand (get) what they had to do to resolve them.

.Before The Wizardry

After The Wizardry

WYSIWYG

Now, on to the tales →

SEE HOW WE STOPPED BEING LATE

Another Missed Deadline

Advertising agencies work in close collaboration with their clients. They work together to develop the ideas for launching a new product and set a schedule for the launch. Then, the agency's back room staff goes to work to develop all of the advertising materials the client wants to accompany the product launch.

This tale is about an advertising agency that develops the specialized printed matter (e.g., fancy brochures, imprinted objects) that the client wants to be able to hand out at a press conference on the day of a new product launch. When these materials are not ready on the day of the launch the client gets very upset. There is always a penalty for missing the date and contract cancellation is always possible.

So, the reason for this tale -- ***The group just missed a launch date for the third time this year.***

About the Group

The production group consists of four teams: Design, Ink, Paper, and Press. The members of each team are all very experienced and expert at what they do. Their products (when they are on time) are world-class.

The Design Team attends the client conferences. They provide designs for the products and specification for the printing and embossing. The Ink Team orders and mixes the inks required. Some of the inks needed to achieve special effects could be classed as exotic. The Paper Team reviews the product specifications from the designers and places orders for the paper. Again, some of the paper needed for special effects can be unusual and may require special ordering. The Press Team is the production team. They take all the inputs from the other teams and produce the final products. The typical time frame for all of this to occur is 90 days.

It sounds very straightforward but it isn't. In order for the process to work well all the components have to work well together. The ink has to be compatible with the paper or it will bleed or smear when being run through the presses. The paper needs to be compatible with the presses so it won't jam or tear when it is being run. The designs are also sensitive to ink and paper issues. Some designs just won't "work" on certain types of papers.

The various team members were aware of all these possible incompatibilities and tried to avoid them. However, whenever they were late it was usually because they got a nasty "incompatibility surprise" somewhere along the way and one or more things would have to be done over with a different design, different materials or different press techniques.

What They Did About It

First, they all agreed that they had to fix their process so they could do a better job of meeting deadlines. They asked for some Wizard help. We got a member from each team into the same room with a big whiteboard. Then, we wrote "Start" at the left edge of the board and "Deliver" on the right edge.

We asked each person to describe to the group everything he or she did between Start and Deliver. The Wizard worked at the chalkboard to capture what was being said in the form of a linear flow of tasks. As each team member described his or her teams' work the Wizard captured and drew that as a separate line. When they were done with their descriptions there were four separate flow charts, one for the work flow of each team.

As the next step, we asked each team member to estimate the amount of time it would normally take to perform each of the tasks on their line. We made sure that their total did not exceed 90 days. Ideally, it would be much less.

What They Began to See

They discovered that there was no evidence of any coordination in any of the task lines. Each unit was working to its own schedule, doing what it thought was required and not talking with the others about what was needed and when in order to meet the delivery date. As a result, delays were being caused by unforeseen mismatches of ink and paper, design and ink, or ink and press. It quickly became apparent to everyone that closer coordination would have to occur.

As they worked with the picture they concluded that there were three things they had to do. First, they had to add some early tasks to discuss and resolve potential incompatibility problems before they occurred. To accomplish this they agreed on a way to coordinate their materials ordering and testing schedules that would substantially reduce the time required for testing. Then they had to figure out how to line up all the tasks that depended on each other in a way that, when done in sequence, they would fit easily into the 90 day maximum schedule. Finally, they had to draw a new version of their picture to reflect their combined schedule.

Life After Headaches

The teams started to use the new chart as a roadmap for their projects. They noticed improvements almost immediately. There were far fewer incompatibilities. Schedule slips became less frequent. Their performance is now pretty consistent. Most important, they have not missed a deadline since the meeting.

This group has recognized that they can do even better. They have also recognized that their process picture might have to change from time-to-time as their clients and suppliers change.

Their process picture is posted on the wall in their hallway. The group now has a regular, once-a-month, Brown Bag lunch meeting where they walk through the process together and discuss potential improvements and agree on whether or not to change their picture. Anyone with an idea for how to make the process work better speaks up and, if they all agree that it would be an improvement, they change the picture.

In these gatherings they also re-affirm that they will be careful to follow the processes because that's the only way they can tell if it is really working.

Wizard Comment

Each team had a very clear idea of what they did but they had never shared that with the other teams. Getting the teams together and getting them to share and try to link their individual process flow charts exposed the situation that was causing the unwanted delays (e.g. the frequent incompatibilities among ink, paper, and design). When the individual teams saw this for the first time, it was a great "Aha!" moment for them. The importance of coordinating their special requirements and schedules for each launch was obvious.

When they all saw it, they all got it.

WYSIWYG

SEE HOW WE STOPPED MAKING MISTAKES

Concerns at the Top

The Sector vice president was concerned. His computer programming group on a government contract in Oak Ridge had been in operation for almost a year and was performing erratically. Their work was generally good but too many of their products were being found defective and were being rejected for re-work. The government contracting officer was concerned because each return added to costs and caused delays in the government work schedule. He asked the Wizard to see what was happening and give him some help in finding a way to fix the situation.

What They Were Doing

The programming group in Oak Ridge consisted of 60 highly qualified programmers. All of them had extensive experience with the government's large data base software system. Their principal job was to process government initiated software change requests.

This work involved reviewing and understanding what functional or performance change was desired, determining what needed to be changed to achieve that, developing the code to do that, testing the code internally and then delivering what they called the "Change Package". Each month they handled an average of 50 such requests. Unfortunately, about once every 10 days or so, a delivered Change Package would be rejected by the government systems staff and would have to be corrected.

How Change Requests Were Processed

Their company standard manual for handling change requests included a detailed flow chart of how it should be done. The process stated in the manual was based on studies of several company operations that were processing change requests for different customers. The manual was developed and issued by the corporate headquarters in Tysons Corner. All of the staff had been trained in the official version of the process.

When we asked them about their process they said that it was written in the Change Process Manual. When we asked for a copy no one seemed to be able to find one. So, we asked them to describe what they really did. They said they could but we would have to talk with everyone because everyone did his work a bit differently.

In practice, each change request was handled individually in the way that the team leader felt would be best, based on "how we did it at the place I worked before" and what he or she remembered about the training and the manual. Because everyone remembered the process in the manual in a slightly different way, as you might expect, a bit of chaos reigned. There were numerous crises and misunderstandings of who should be doing what with each change.

Getting to See

Since there were three teams we asked each to develop a high level flow chart of their process for handling the requests. When we compared them we found different steps, different nomenclature, and different understandings of the tasks involved in each of the blocks. However, there was enough similarity that it appeared that the differences among the various approaches could be harmonized into a process that might work well for everyone. They agreed to agree on a single version.

The way they approached it was interesting and effective. The leaders of the three teams worked together with sticky notes on a wall to get agreement on the basic steps involved in the life cycle of a change. Then, they got a really large sheet of paper (i.e., 15 feet long and 3 feet from top to bottom). They transferred the flow of their basic process from the wall to the paper and posted the foundation diagram in the hallway in a place that everyone passed through at least twice a day. They also put a box of sticky notes and some pens nearby and asked everyone to post comments and suggestions that would make the chart better and would reflect exactly what they were doing.

Now All Could See

Once a week the team leaders revisited and updated the chart to reflect the comments on the process trying to reconcile differences. Within a few weeks the comments converged and an agreed process began to emerge. When we returned and asked to see their process they pointed to their chart proudly and said, ***"This is it and we all are following it".***

As evidence of that, they showed us their development folders. Each one had a list of the change request life cycle process steps printed on it and a place for initials to be applied as each step was completed and signed off by both the sender and the receiver. All of the relevant documentation was recorded in each folder.

We then asked how that compared to the corporate standard. That sparked another review of their process versus the corporate standard and they discovered major differences. At this point the team ownership of "their" life cycle was so strong that they agreed to recommend their process as a replacement for the corporate standard – and it was ultimately accepted.

Seeing and Getting the Process

The beneficial effects of having their own, visible life cycle were felt almost immediately. There were fewer misunderstandings and fewer crises. Team members could now take vacations and someone could fill in for them because the work to be done at each stage was specified and would be done by the substitute just the same way that the original assignee would have done it. As turnover occurred, new team members were introduced to the chart and shown where they fit in the various processes. The chart was kept on the wall as a constant reference.

Number of Days Since the Last Rejected Change Package

152

Some smiles began to appear on the faces of the team members. They told us, "It's good that we are now doing everything the same way. All the uncertainty we used to have has gone away. Every day I come to work and I know exactly what I have to do today and when I've done it I can go home. No more crises and no more unscheduled overtime!"

The Big Payoff

Once the process smoothed out, the frequency of product rejections dropped significantly. As an incentive to keep the reject rate down, the senior manager posted a sign above the big chart and had the team leaders keep it updated.

The last time we visited, they proudly pointed to their sign. No rejects for over five months!

Wizard Comment

Some problems are too big to be solved on small paper. In this tale, the group had a long-complex process and a tough problem. This was a "big piece of paper" problem. They started to solve it on the wall with sticky notes that they could manipulate until they reached agreement. Then, they recorded their standard approach on the paper for all to see – and improve over time.

Getting the group to see and resolve their differences on their big wall chart:

- Established a consistent process
- Provided a constant reminder of the process
- Greatly reduced misunderstandings and errors
- Improved performance consistency
- Facilitated training new staff
- Fostered a sense of teamwork

Working together to build the process chart was a great team-building experience. The participants developed a sense of shared ownership of the process that they had developed, defended and drawn. When they all saw it, they all got it together – in more ways than one.

SEE TIME IN A USEFUL WAY

SEE ANNE SEE AND SEIZE SNIPPETS OF TIME

SEE FRED SHRINK OVERTIME

TIME

What very mysterious things days are. Sometimes they fly by, and other times they seem to last forever, yet they are all exactly twenty-four hours. There's quite a lot we don't know about them.

-- Melanie Benjamin, *Alice I Have Been, 2010*

Time is what we want most, but use worst.

-- William Penn

If you want to make good use of your time, you've got to know what's most important and then give it all you've got.

– Lee Iacocca

You will never find time for anything. If you want time, you must make it.

-- Charles Buxton

There is never enough time, unless you're serving it.

-- Malcolm Forbes

SEE TIME IN A USEFUL WAY

The next two tales are about two people for whom 24 hour days are too short. Neither one seems to be able to get done all the things they have to do or should be doing within the time available. They both work hard and long, eat at their desks while they work and sleep less than Mom always told them they should. Even with all that, they still can't get it everything done when they need to.

You may find that you have similar problems. Anne gets a lot done but there are some important things she should be doing to build her business that she never seems to be able to get to. She needs to find a way to squeeze those things into her day.

Fred's problem seems to be missing deadlines. The project leaders who rely on him for critical pieces of software for their programs frequently find that what they told Fred they needed yesterday won't be ready until tomorrow or later.

Both Anne and Fred were desperate. In their tales you will find out how they came to see what was happening to their time and how they arrived at a solution to their problem.

> **He who every morning plans the transaction of the day and follows out the plan, carries a thread that will guide him through the labyrinth of the most busy life.**
>
> **– Victor Hugo**

SEE ANNE SEE AND SEIZE SNIPPETS OF TIME

Anne is a real estate agent who specializes in commercial sales. She learned her business by watching other agents. She was mentored by one of the older ones through the first several months. She did well but always felt rushed and always had a hard time fitting all the phone calls she had to make into her day. With the phone calls as a priority, she often had to work late to get all her other work done.

When we first talked, Anne said she desperately wanted to find a way to make better use of her time. She had been thinking about what she was doing and it was all sort of a blur. She was always busy (e.g., meetings, paperwork, calls, conferences) and she wasn't able to see any "empty" moments. Anne felt that if she could find such moments she would be able to squeeze into them some of the things she now had to do after the end of the normal workday.

In our first discussion we talked about the importance of being fully aware of (i.e., "seeing") the details of what she was doing. We agreed that that was the key to finding ways to make better use of one's time. We both felt that when she could see the whole picture she would be able to spot some unproductive and wasted moments and would be able to put them to better use.

Setting the Time Trap

Anne agreed to take a few minutes each morning to prepare a "Today Sheet". She would list her scheduled appointments, follow-up telephone calls and other planned tasks for the day in the order in which she expected to do them. She would also estimate the time she thought each task was likely to take.

Anne also agreed to take a few minutes at the end of the day to record the actual amount of time each planned task took and to record what she did with the "free" time if the task took less time than planned. Anne understood that is was going to require some effort but she resolved to do this for a couple of weeks and then we would take a look at the results together to see what was happening. We both hoped that when she could see the spare moments she could get them and make better use of them. Put simply, what she could see, she could get.

Checking the Trap

As Anne got into it she began to realize that things didn't always go as planned every day. There were variations. Sometimes some of the things she did took less time than she thought they would. A meeting might get cancelled or getting some rental documents ready might take less time than usual. Those situations seemed to yield what she was looking for – the "extra" moments that she might capture and use.

After two weeks of tracking we reviewed her notes and discovered several things. First, there were many unplanned "free" moments that occurred every day. We called those moments in time "snippets".

Second, she saw that what she was usually doing in those snippets was checking her e-mail and the latest news. Neither of those activities was very productive. She really did not need to do these any more than twice a day and here she was, doing them every time she had a free moment. When she added up the time she was spending on those, the total came to almost an hour a day of time that might be put to better use if she could find a way.

We began to look for useful things that she had to do that were small enough to fit into those snippets of time that she had discovered. She found a number of things that could be done at any time during the day and usually only took a couple of minutes each. She made a list.

- Next Day Prep – Reviewing contact sheets for next day appointments
- Inventory Walk – Reviewing the list of available properties
- Lead Follow-up – Calling new leads
- "Bird Dogging" - Prospecting for leads by calling friends, , associates
- Making Follow-up calls to clients to whom she had sold something

As we reviewed the list we agreed that the first three things were so important that she should schedule time to do them. The last two items were the important things for which she never seemed to have enough time. Maybe we could find out how to fit those in to the spare moments.

Preparing to Use Snippets of Time

The problem with trying to make better use of time snippets is that you can't be sure when they will occur. They just pop up and you have to be ready to take advantage of them. You can't predict when a meeting will run short, traffic will be less than expected, or any of the other "snippet producers" that may occur.

Anne figured out that in order to be ready to do make use of the snippet time she would have to have a handy list of potential calls that she could make when the opportunities arose. So, she added a few minutes to her schedule each morning to update her call lists for "Bird Dogging" and Follow Ups with past clients. She kept those with her throughout the day and used them whenever she had a spare moment.

Over the next few weeks Anne found that changing what she was doing was not as easy as she thought. The siren call of e-mail and the news feeds was very strong and she had to remind herself to go to her call lists first – before getting distracted. However, as she gradually worked into the routine she began to see that she was making more calls and getting good results from that.

Anne was convinced. She continued to use her Today Sheet as a window into her activities. It helped her see what she was doing and "get" (understand) where and how she could make what she was doing work better.

Wizard Comment

At the outset, Anne knew there must be moments that she could capture and use more productively but she could not see them. Anne had to find a way to make time visible. She did that by starting and maintaining a record of her time – how she planned to spend it and how she actually spent it.

Anne's daily records provided snapshots of her activities and enabled her to see and analyze the details of her work patterns and habits. Once she could see the "snippets of time", Anne was able to change her habits and get prepared to capture them when they occurred.

Anne's written "Today Sheet" was a tabular record, not a flow chart like Sarah's, but it was still a case of "writing something down so she could change it". Sound familiar?

SEE FRED SHRINK OVERTIME

About Fred

Fred is one member of a small group of technical experts who design and build specialized products that include both hardware and software. Fred is a "super coder", a very special kind of computer programmer.

The computer code that Fred writes is a key part of most of the active projects in his workgroup. He comes to work early and leaves late most days and his output is always good.

If you ask Fred to do something he will always agree to take it on and he will add it to his list. Fred usually has at least eight or nine things on his personal "To Do" list on his computer. Fred's list is in order by "When Requested". A lot of the dates are very close, and Fred considers them all to be "Urgent". Every morning Fred comes in and looks at his list on his computer and gets to work on the next item on the list. Fred works on the items as fast as he can and turns out a huge amount of work.

Tasking Fred

New requirements come in daily from customers. Some of those are new requirements for new products and others are for modifications of requirements for products already in progress. The team usually has about 15 such projects going at any one time. It is vital for these products to be available at the time they are scheduled to be delivered.

A project leader who needs something from Fred for his project figures out what it was he needs and then discusses it with Fred. Fred, as always, says "I can do that". Then, Fred enters the task on his list. Project leaders always consider the tasks in their projects as the most important, and the most urgent. There is an old saying that has been translated into many languages. One of the more colorful versions is: "Every monkey in the eyes of his mother is a gazelle". Every project leader tells Fred that his task (his monkey) is the most critical. So, each task joins Fred's queue of baby gazelles on his list. As far as Fred knows, all of the tasks are ***"urgent, important, needed as soon as possible",*** so he works on them as fast as he can.

Is Fred The Problem?

Lately, the group had been missing deadlines and the leaders whose projects were late were saying that they were being held up by Fred's stuff. The number of missed deadlines was serious and the group decided to try to fix it. There was no viable way open to refuse any of the incoming requirements. They could not reduce the group's workload. So, they had to figure out how to get Fred's work when they needed it to complete their projects on schedule.

Fred was very productive. Fred was already working a lot of overtime and they did not want to work him any harder. They thought about getting more Freds. However, Fred's skills were truly unique so that option was out. All the things Fred was tasked to do he could, eventually, get done. He could turn out as much product as needed every day. The problem was that some of the things he was doing really weren't needed right away and others, farther down his list, were needed yesterday.

There was an overall schedule posted and maintained for all of the projects. Each project lead managed his own project's schedule and pressed to get the work done on time to meet the current schedule. However, as the Wizard pointed out to them, there was no schedule for the one critical item that affected almost every project – the various tasks they had asked Fred to accomplish.

WYSIWYG to the Rescue

All of the project leads were assuming that Fred was doing what they had asked him to do. None of them had any idea of what other work was on Fred's list. So, we asked Fred to print out his list (Fred's Sked). You can see what it looked like.

Fred's list on the computer was in order by when he was asked to do the task. To get a different look, we asked him to sort it by due date with the nearest dates at the top. That gave us a much different picture.

Fred's Original List

Fred's Sked		Today = 2 September
TASKS	**Estimated Hours**	**Due Date**
New Module – Project C	24	3-Sep
Fix Security – Project A	28	6-Sep
Adjust parameters – Project B	22	10-Sep
New Module – Project X	22	4-Sep
New Module – Project Y	30	8-Sep
Change Exit Report – Project C	18	12-Sep
Delete Useless Code – Project B	12	20-Sep
New Module – Project - S	14	16-Sep

Fred's Sorted List

Fred's Sked		Today = 2 September
TASKS	**Estimated Hours**	**Due Date**
New Module – Project C	24	3-Sep
New Module – Project X	22	4-Sep
Fix Security – Project A	28	6-Sep
This Week Total	**74**	
New Module – Project Y	30	8-Sep
Adjust parameters – Project B	22	10-Sep
Next Week Total	**52**	
Change Exit Report – Project C	18	12-Sep
New Module – Project - S	14	16-Sep
Delete Useless Code – Project B	12	20-Sep
Coming Up	**44**	

Now All Could See

Now, for the first time, we could all see what tasks Fred was working on to try to meet the deadlines – and so could Fred. We could clearly see that there were not enough hours in Fred's work week (and overtime) to do all the work that had been requested to be completed for each week.

It now was very clear that Fred was way overbooked. He had 74 hours of work due this week and 52 hours that the project leads wanted to have done by the end of next week. Something had to give. Now the three project leaders had to talk and agree to adjust their deadlines.

This was an eye-opener for the project leads and for Fred. Fred already knew he was taking on too much but he didn't think it was his place to tell a project lead that he had to change his schedule. His job was to just get all the work done as fast as he could.

Aha! – The Problem Isn't Fred

We concluded that the problem wasn't Fred. The problem was that the project leads had not been looking at Fred's existing commitments before asking him to do new work. The problem was theirs, not Fred's.

Fred and the Project leads needed a simple method to keep Fred's schedule visible and to support the orderly negotiations of deadlines. They found that the "Fred's Sked" spreadsheet worked well. Now Fred keeps the current version of that posted on the outside wall of his cubicle. The project leads consult it regularly as they work on their project schedules to integrate Fred's tasks with all their other tasks.

Wizard Comment

The problem was a group problem but the group could not see the overload on Fred's schedule. Printing out and posting the current version of the Fred Sked on the portal to Fred's cubicle exposed the problem and provided a mechanism for the Project Leaders to see potential scheduling problems and resolve them before they became a problem. When they could see the problem they could fix it.

Now Fred never has to struggle to get 70 or 80+ hours of work done in a week. He still usually works more than 40 hours a week but he is happier now because the negotiated deadlines are much more reasonable and he is meeting them.

SEE HOW WE HELP OTHERS SEE

SEE CUSTOMERS BECOME WAIT-LESS

SEE AND FIX COMMUNITY PROBLEMS

SEE OPPORTUNITIES TO GIVE AND SAVE

Seeing, in the finest and broadest sense, means using your senses, your intellect, and your emotions. It means encountering your subject matter with your whole being. It means looking beyond the labels of things and discovering the remarkable world around you.

– Freeman Patterson

SEE HOW WE HELP OTHERS SEE

Getting Others to See

In the previous sections you saw tales about individuals who found different ways to see what they were doing and how they got an understanding of how they could improve their performance.

Anne was able to see where she had spare moments in her work day and got ideas on how to make better use of them. Fred's project managers were finally able to see why he was always behind schedule and got a way to fix that.

And so it is with the tales to come. In each of these, the crucial part is some technique for helping people discover and document situations in ways that will benefit them.

The Gap Method for Stimulating Action

There is a strong urge in many humans to try to solve problems. When these people see a gap or a hole in something they feel compelled to try to fill the gap. This is the basis for what we call the "Gap Method for Stimulating Action". To help people see and act on these gaps you have to arrange things so that the gap stands out. Once they see the gaps their interest in filling them will be stimulated and action should follow.

If you doubt the strength of this impulse you can try this example. At some place where a number of others will be passing by, write on a whiteboard or put up a sticky note showing the following:

Leave it there for a while with a pencil, marker or crayon nearby. Check it later to see what has happened.

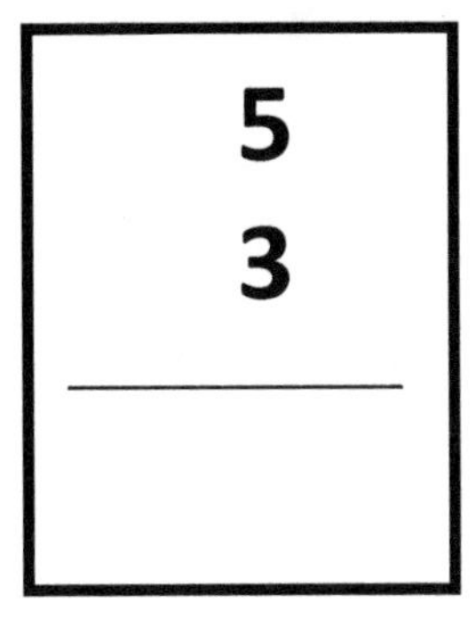

The usual result is that someone will have filled in a plus, minus, or multiplication sign and will have completed the operation. *(You may have had that urge when you were posting it.)* If you were to ask people about the note, few would say that it was just a 5 and a 3 and a line. Most would have seen it as an arithmetic problem and those who did would have felt an urge to complete the problem and may have done so.

--------------------------- ***What did you think when you saw the 5 and 3?***

Mind the Gap

The lesson from this is, if you have a job to be done, find a way to display it in such a way that people will perceive it as a gap that needs to be filled. Just getting someone to see it as a gap may be enough to draw action. When applying this method in a business situation you can include an incentive to fill the gap by identifying someone to be responsible for filling it and making the gap and the assignment public. That will add peer pressure to the incentive for filling the gap.

In this section we will show you a number of examples of how the gap method has been applied to help some other people see gaps and get the problem and take appropriate action.

What You   Is What You Get

(See! -- It Works. I bet you filled in the gap.)

SEE CUSTOMERS BECOME WAIT-LESS

This Tale is About Ralph

It's always nice to meet and talk with a bright, innovative person. From the Wizard's standpoint it was really great to meet Ralph and hear about how he was able to see and implement a practical, new way to deal with his waiting line problem.

Ralph is the manager of a military commissary in a town that has a large population of military families. For most of these families the commissary is their supermarket for all their major food and other consumable items. The store is well-stocked, clean, and well run. The only complaints that customers have are about long waits in line at checkout. That has been a problem. There have been far too many complaints about long waits.

About the Commissary

The commissary has six checkout lines. Four are always open and the other two are opened during peak periods by staff members who do double duty. They staff the registers during the peaks and during off-peak times they stock shelves. Ralph does not have any room in his budget to hire more staff.

What Ralph Has Been Doing

Ralph has been responding to the complaints by reading up on better ways to handle waiting lines. Some of the ideas he has read about include such things as double-siding the checker stations so that the checker can ring someone up on one side and then switch to ringing up the other side while the first customer gathers up what they bought and moves on. There were some other ideas about speeding up the checkers, but none of those looked as if they could work for his situation.

Most of what he read was focused on ways to distract the people in line to keep them from noticing how long they were waiting. That's the Disney approach – provide something for the customers to see and do while they are waiting. He tried several of the ideas but they did not seem to be well received. Ralph thought that, short of his learning magic tricks or doing a song-and-dance routine there was not much he could do.

The complaints continued at their usual pace. What could Ralph do?

What Ralph Saw

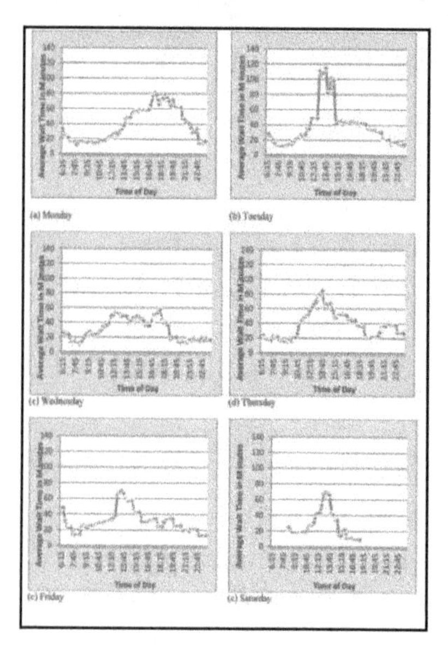

When Ralph went back over the research again he saw that all of the ideas focused on crowds that were already at the amusement park or store and were lining up for rides or to checkout. When the crowds were large, the lines and the waits were long. When the crowds were small the lines and waits were short.

"Aha!" He thought: "Maybe I can figure out how to keep my crowds small but still take care of everyone who wants to come. Perhaps I can find a way to move their shopping times from peak to off-peak times.

How Ralph Helped His Customers See a Better Time to Shop

Ralph knew when the peaks and off-peaks occurred and when the waiting lines were long. He had data on the number of people in line at each half hour for every day of the week. He had been collecting the data for the past three months and the pattern was pretty consistent. He converted that to waiting time by multiplying it by the average time it took to complete a checkout, a figure he had computed earlier.

Ralph figured that if he could show these charts to the shoppers they would see opportunities to change their shopping habits by coming to the commissary at different times to avoid the long waiting times. If they did that, the peaks would smooth out and the longest times would grow shorter. He had some special racks made and posted the prior week's charts alongside each checkout line where those waiting would have a good chance to study them.

What Happened Next

The customers now had something pretty interesting to do while they were waiting. They could see and think about what the charts were telling them. As they studied the charts some of the customers began to see what they could do to shorten their waiting time.

They began to come at different times and the lines representing the waiting times on the charts began to smooth out showing shorter waits.

Ralph benefitted in two ways. His patrons could see that he was working on the problems and, better yet, the wait times were getting shorter. After six months, the complaints ceased.

Wizard Comment

Ralph did two important things. First, he figured out that the solution to the problem was getting patrons to spread out their arrival times. Then, Ralph selected the right data and presented it to his patrons in a way that made it easy for them to see the problem and share in its solution.

When they saw it, they got it and
"they all lived happily ever after".

Post Script: There are now numerous smartphone and tablet apps that provide timely waiting time information for travelers. One can now easily see how long the wait lines will be at airports and train stations and many other locations and plan departure times accordingly. Maybe they got the idea from Ralph.

WYSIWYG

DATA

A person who is gifted sees the essential point and leaves the rest as surplus.-

- Thomas Carlyle, Scottish Writer

Big data's fine; the right data's a game changer.

-- Andy Palmer -- Vertica Systems and VoltDB founder

SEE AND FIX COMMUNITY PROBLEMS

Now You See Them

Every neighborhood has eyesores. You see them all the time – trash piles, abandoned cars or toys, potholes – whatever. They are all too easy to see. What's hard to see is the way to get rid of them.

Whenever you see an eyesore, you say to yourself that "somebody" ought to get rid of them. But, who is the right somebody and how can you get them to see this eyesore and cure it? The usual somebodies are various local government agencies, civic associations, service clubs (Lions, Rotary), and eco-friendly volunteer organizations. At this point you are stymied. You don't know which one is the right one. Even if you have a pretty good idea you still have to find out how to report the eyesore to them.

Now You Don't

Those organizations have different, but related, problem. They have resources to fix eyesores but they generally don't have sufficient resources to go looking for them. They are happy to go cure eyesores promptly, when reported, but it's hard to fix something that you can't see.

So, we have two populations, each with a problem in relation to eyesores. One group can see the eyesores but can't easily see how to report them. The other group can't readily see the eyesores but stands ready to cure them whenever they can see them.

What's The Big Idea?

At a recent Chautauqua presentation, Megan Smith, Google VP for Innovation, told the Wizard about a conference in England a few years ago called ***Silicon Valley Comes to the UK***. The conference was open to university students and others and included an **"App-athon"**. The government released a lot of government data, encouraged the attendees to develop ways to make use of the data, and held a contest to pick the best applications. One of the top winners was, aptly, called **"Eye Sore"**.

The developers described how their app idea would work. You would see something that was a problem in your community, an eye sore. Then you would take a photo of it, post in a community-collaborative place, and then anyone could go fix the problem. You could go fix it and get credit and everyone would see what you had done. A company could pay money for the work and could get grant credit, or the community could vote the worst problems up and ask the town council to fix the top five. It was a great idea!

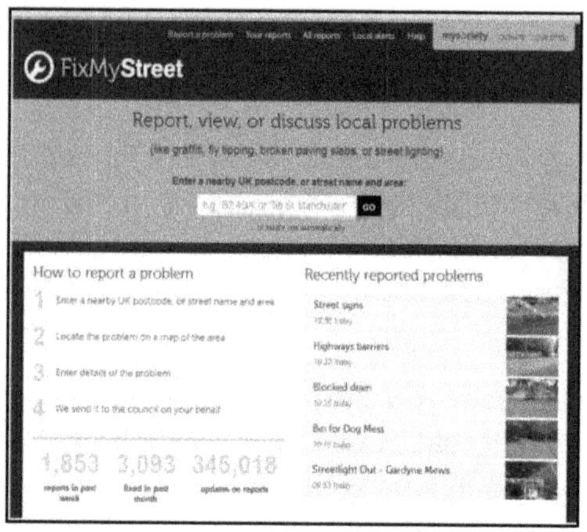

Now What?

In England the original idea has come to life in a number of government and private apps. FixMyStreet.com, gives residents in local councils a hassle-free way of reporting needed street repairs, instead of muddling through a gamut of Web sites. **FixMyStreet** relays user-generated complaints to the right office, and provides a community forum, following up with an e-mail to ask how the complaint was handled. Local governments in Norway, India and Canada are copying the model.

In the U.S., a start-up was founded by a group of four New Haven, Conn. residents with a knack for software engineering, design and entrepreneurship. They were inspired to launch **SeeClickFix** after seeing **FixMyStreet**.

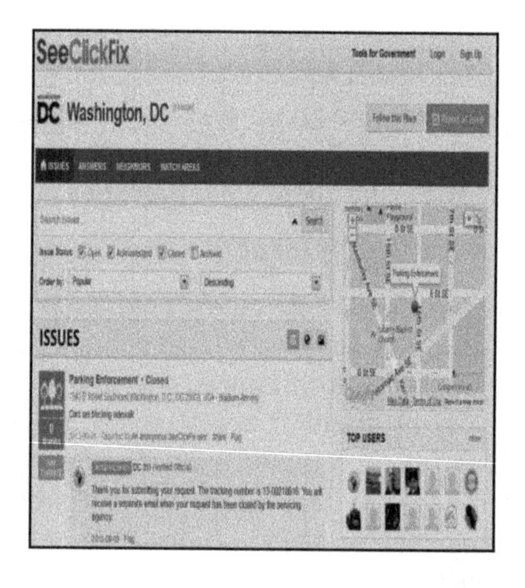

Lately, the **SeeClickFix** guys have garnered national media attention and were profiled by Voice of America (en Espanol).

SeeClickFix works with Google maps and government agency software to provide an extended version of what we used to call a pothole tracker. These systems seek reports about abandoned cars or homes, malfunctioning traffic signals or sanitation violations.

"Community empowerment" comes in three easy steps, as the name implies:

See – See a non-emergency issue in your neighborhood

Click – open a ticket describing the issue and what can be done to resolve it

Fix – publicly report the issue to everyone for resolution

Benefits

The eyesore types of applications are a good example of expanding the way government data is shared with the public. In the past, eyesore reports were stashed in agency files and invisible to everyone except the workers in the agency to which they had been reported. Now that they can be seen by all there is an opportunity for others, outside the agency, to become aware of and assist in the eyesore curing efforts. The end result is that more organizations can be involved in the eyesore curing process and, presumably, more eyesores will be cured faster.

The existence of these internet applications has significantly eased the problem we mentioned at the outset – trying to find out where and how one should report an eyesore. One no longer has to search through the phone book to look for the listing for the right agency or organization and place a call to their Help Desk. Now, if you see an eyesore and want to report it, you can take a picture, bring up the app on your phone, and report it. What you have seen will then be routed to the system where everyone can see it. Then, if you are someone with the resources to cure eyesores, when you see the problem you get what needs to be done and can get started doing it.

Perhaps the greatest benefit of this type of application is the strengthening of the public-private partnership in local communities. Members of the community now have an easier way to interact with their local agencies and organizations and everyone can see what needs to be done and what is getting done to maintain and improve the local environment.

Wizard Comment

When you use technology creatively to link government with the public citizens, here's what you get:

The public sees:

They see an easy way to report Eyesores and to follow progress in curing them.

The eyesore curers see:

They now can easily see all the eyesores we see.

And, the eyesores get fixed!

WYSIWYG

SEE OPPORTUNITIES TO GIVE AND SAVE

The Lure of the Gap

It is instructive and fun to recall the many ways you have been lured into doing something by the hidden urge to fill a gap. Who does the luring? The people who want you to do something. How do they do it? They set you up by creating a situation that allows (or compels you) to see the gap and conveys a sense of urgency in getting it filled.

The following mini-tales are examples of gaps that the Wizard has seen being used to spark action.

Collecting Quarters

A few years ago a daughter gave the Wizard a copy of **The Official United States Mint 50 State Quarters® Collector's Map.** This was custom-designed and produced for the Mint with the collector in mind. The blurb that came with it said:

> ***This colorful and highly informative collector's album has many features that make it a fun and educational tool for a child, adult or the whole family! A topographical state map of the United States with push-fit holders in which to collect all 50 State Quarters® from circulation. What fun for a child (or you!) to hunt for and collect each new quarter out of pocket change!***

Wow! Fifty gaps to fill. Who could resist the opportunity to fill those push-fit holes? The Wizard quickly became a collector and eagerly awaited the scheduled release of the new quarter for each state.

Then, in tiny print at the bottom of the chart is this little note expanding the gap:

> ***Option to customize maps for collection of either Denver or Philadelphia mintmarks. In reality, there will be 100 quarters, not just 50! Unfolds to over*** *3 feet in length!*

How many gaps can they create to spur sales?

United Way

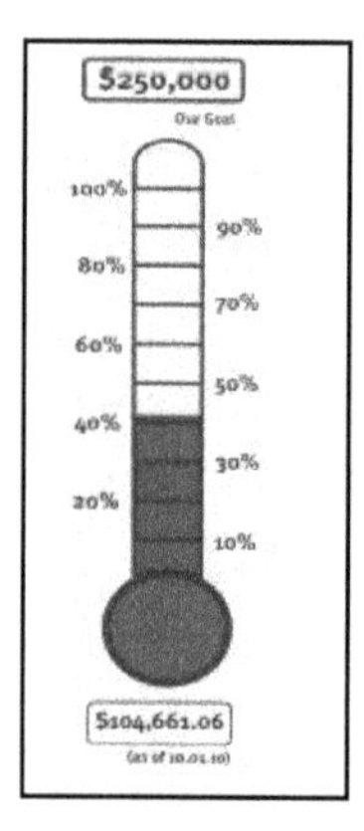

At one time or another everyone (including the Wizard) gets tapped to do some fundraising. The thermometer chart is the standard display used to help people see the gap to be filled. The Pie Chart also works, but is less effective. The gap is less apparent.

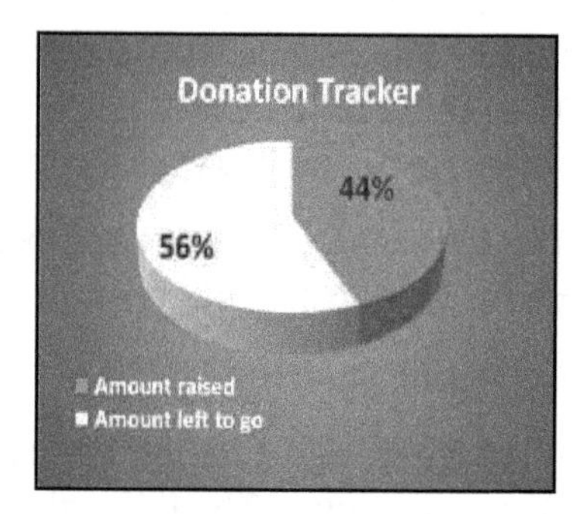

Adding a Human Touch

All of these show a gap but they are not very compelling. They do not automatically stir the emotions and the desire to give. Adding a human factor – When you see a hungry child, the need for money to feed the child – makes the gap personal and easier to see.

This photo from a donation promo shows two children cradling the goats they have been given by donors. It makes it easy to see the value that will accrue from participating in the "Give a Goat for Christmas" program.

Kids with kids – How can you beat that!

Business Gaps

When the Wizard is working with groups to help them define their business goals he puts on the board an empty chart and asks the participants to fill it in.

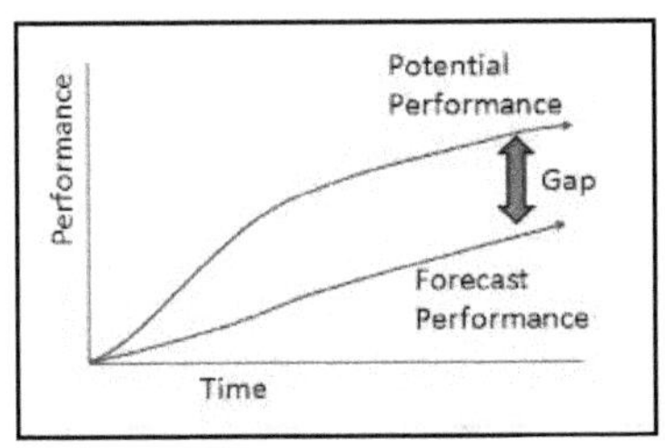

Meeting Goals

When the Wizard is trying to encourage groups to improve their performance he uses a chart like this and asks the members of the group how they will improve their performance and bridge the gap.

Wizard Comment

The Gap method can be a powerful tool. The key is being able to present the gap in a way that makes it easy for the viewer to see the opportunity to act.

... and don't forget one of the Wizard's favorites, a sign in front of a church that is intended to encourage attendance –

CH __ __ CH

What's Missing?

U R

WYSIWYG

Whenever you want to achieve something, keep your eyes open, concentrate and make sure you know exactly what it is you want. No one can hit their target with their eyes closed.

— Paulo Coelho, The Devil and Miss Prym

SEE WHAT'S REALLY IMPORTANT

SEE HOW TO LOOK LESS AND SEE MORE

SEE FUTURE PROBLEMS NOW

Getting organized in the normal routines of life and finishing little projects you've started is an important first step toward realizing larger goals.

If you can't get a handle on the small things, how will you ever get it together to focus on the big things?

-- Joyce Meyer

SEE WHAT'S REALLY IMPORTANT

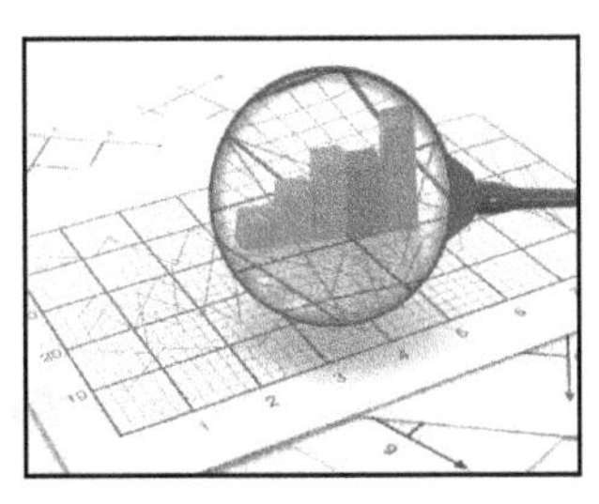

Sometimes what we really need to see is hiding before our eyes. In an information rich world it is very difficult to sort through all the data to isolate what is important for any given situation. What we need may be buried among rows and columns in a spreadsheet, obscured by wordy descriptions in a written document or presented in a busy chart.

The tales in this section provide two examples in which those involved were able to *narrow their* focus and zero in on the information that was critical to their success.

The first tale is about how one innovative police officer found a way to improve his department's stolen car recovery rate by looking at fewer cars.

In the second tale you will read about a project team that was ignoring little indicators of future major problems until their manager focused their attention with a little piece of red string.

Both tales illustrate the point, that one of the police officers made, **"Sometimes you can see more by looking at less".**

WYSIWYG

Now, on to the next tales →

The News

FBI'S 'MOST-WANTED FUGITIVES' NAMED

SEE HOW TO LOOK LESS AND SEE MORE

Morning Roll Call

At the morning Roll Call a few years ago, the Indianapolis Chief of Police spoke to his patrol officers about his frustration with their inability to locate stolen cars. He mentioned the stolen car listing that showed the make, model, year, color, and license plate data for the 128 cars currently being sought. Then he pointed out that the recovery rate was really very poor – only 1 or 2 a week – and they should be getting a lot more. At this rate, the list was continuing to grow because the theft rate was outstripping the recovery rate. The public, especially the citizen's whose cars had been stolen, were getting pretty upset so they would have to find a better way to spot and recover the cars on the list. He asked for ideas on ways to improve on what they were doing.

Meeting with the Chief

The next week one of the patrol officers asked for and got time with the Chief to present his idea. When they met, he told the Chief his view of the problem they were having in spotting the stolen cars. He said that the list they were getting at the Roll Call each morning was too long. As they were riding on patrol and looking at cars along the way there was no good way to match up in their head all the cars they were seeing with all the data on the cars on the list. He said that what they needed to do was find a way to better focus their attention on what they should be looking for. He reminded the Chief how good the patrols were in finding cars when they were just looking for one at a time like when they got an APB to look for a **"Red, 4 door Kia, with a license number ending in 534, just seen leaving a robbed 7-11 on Earle Street".** They almost always got these quickly and it was because they could easily remember exactly what they should be looking for.

He told the Chief that his idea was to do something that would narrow down the stolen car list to help make it easier for the patrols to focus on -- something special to look for. He thought something like the FBI's very successful "10 Most Wanted List" would help. He and the Chief discussed how that had begun and why it worked so well.

How "Top Ten" Helps Us See

One of the FBI's longest-running programs — the Ten Most Wanted Fugitives — was the result of a newspaper story. In 1949, International News Service reporter James F. Donovan asked the FBI: "Who are the 10 toughest guys you are looking for?" The FBI gave him a list. Donovan's front-page report in *The Washington Daily News* displayed photos of four escapees, three con men, two murder suspects and a bank robber. The list was a hit. It clearly focused the public's attention on the really bad guys and people began to spot them and call in tips to the FBI that would lead to them to the people on the list. Some of the fugitives were captured quickly as a result.

The idea, outlined by the officer, was to create something like a "10 Most Wanted" car list for the patrol officers to use as a target listing instead of the big spreadsheet. He suggested that they could select which cars to focus on by selecting some very visible characteristic that would be easy to see. His choice was car color. Each day he would select and print out from the list a short list that would include just the stolen cars of one specific color. Because of all the variations in color the list of those of just one color would usually include only about 10-12 cars. Then, the patrol officers could focus their attention on just the cars of the "color of the day" as they rode patrol.

This approach would be a lot easier for them. They only had to look carefully at cars of the specified color and they only had to keep in mind the license numbers or other data about the cars of that color as they thought about a match. The Chief thought this might work and gave the go-ahead.

"Ten Most Wanted" Cars

Starting the next week, each morning at Roll Call, the patrols were told the "Stolen Car Color of the Day" and given a list of the data for the stolen cars of that color. Then, they went off to their normal patrols. The results were striking. Recovery rates went up immediately. The patrols began to pick up 3 or 4 a week instead of 1 or 2 a week. The department continued the program and it became a model for other jurisdictions.

The Rest of The Story

Indianapolis police officers today are using a new scanning device that can quickly identify stolen cars. It uses a pair of cameras attached to a squad car that scans license plates and compares them in less than a second to a nationwide FBI database of reported stolen vehicles. The new system scanners can also help the police find cars that are wanted for other reasons.

Wizard Comment

One of the officers talked about the benefits that he felt that he got from their early effort based on the "Most Wanted" approach to focusing. He said that when he only had to look at cars of the color of the day he had more time to take a closer look at all the other things that he is required to be looking for. He said that learning to focus like that made him a better policeman.

The officer summed up his experience for the Wizard by saying:

"I've learned to look less and see more."

Focusing tightly on the important data was the key to this tale.

WYSIWYG

A	600
L L	480
I S G O I N G	240
V E R Y W E L L	120
E X C E P T F O R	80
A N O V E R U N A N D	40
A B I G S C H E D U L E S L I P	20
N O W W E C A N S E E I T	20

SEE FUTURE PROBLEMS NOW

Things Were Going Great

The Wizard was part of a team assembled to replace an old satellite image processing system with all new hardware and software. Our team included six of us on the government management team and a total of 33 contractor staff from three different companies. The contractors were specialized: one for software; one for the computing hardware; and one for displays. We were starting an eighteen month schedule. My job was to help the Project Manager resolve any technical issues that came up and to assist in monitoring progress.

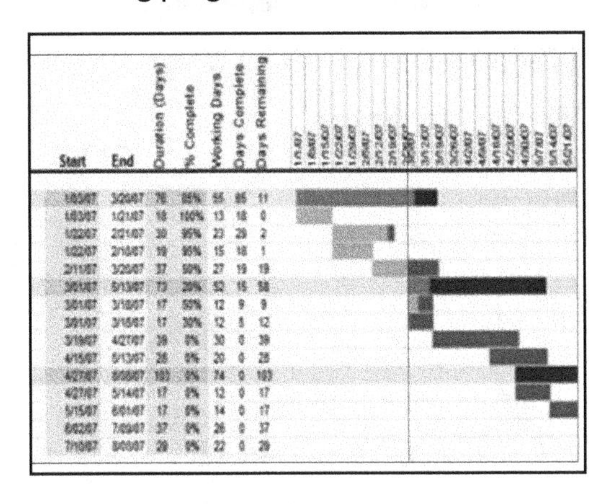

We had only been working for a few weeks so far and, on the surface, things seemed to be going great. However, the Project Manager and I had a vague feeling that the project was beginning to slip. We had both recently read a US Air Force study of project schedule slips. It showed that projects that were behind schedule at the 15% mark never recovered their slippage. Worse yet, those that were behind at this point usually slipped even more. That made us nervous because we were now just about at the 15% point, the third month of an 18 month schedule. If we had slippages now we could already be in trouble.

"We're Doing Fine"

The project had been planned by the combined team and the schedule and tasking was recorded on-line in Microsoft Project©. We had a "War Room" with a giant Gantt chart on the wall showing the detailed task schedules and progress for each of the contractors posted.

The chart followed standard Gantt chart conventions. Each task was represented by a horizontal hollow bar that ran from the scheduled start date to the scheduled finish date. As each task was completed the hollow bar was filled in and the bar would appear as solid black.

We had regular meetings in the War Room on various matters and the current version of the chart was always there as a backdrop but was not usually discussed. We had special meetings every other week to review progress. The Gantt chart served as a general background for the discussions. Sitting around the conference table in the War Room each contractor Task Manager would report that things were going well. As they reported, however, we kept hearing, “One or two tasks might be lagging but we’re ahead on the others so, we’re fine”. After two or three meetings like this the PM decided that we had to find out in more detail what was really happening.

A Three Foot Piece of Red String

All it took to highlight our problems was a three foot piece of red string. How could such a simple thing as a piece of string become a powerful project management tool? Here’s how.

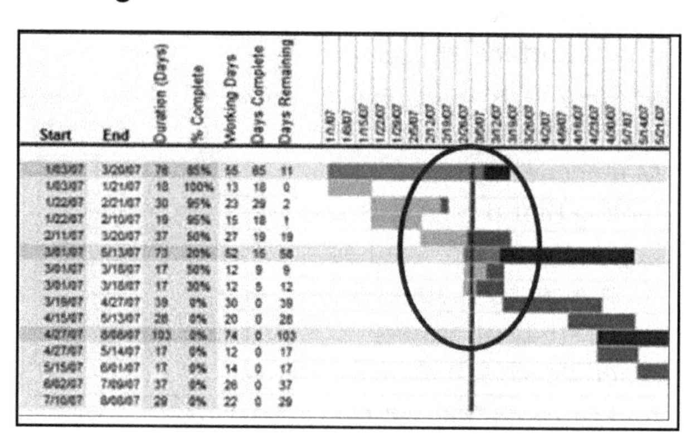

The String Effect

At the beginning of the meeting on the 15th of November we went to the project Gantt chart and fixed the top of the string to the 15 November mark on the schedule line. We ran the string straight down to the bottom and taped it in place. We called the piece of string the “Today Line”.

Then, we called all the Task Managers in and reviewed the chart details with them.

It was now clearly apparent that any task that was supposed to be done by “Today” that was to the left of “The Today Line” and was not shown to be done was late and we could see where and how many there were. There were quite a few. Now, with their late tasks so clearly highlighted the task managers had to provide details on their slippages and how much effort would be required to finish each unfinished task.

Likewise, any completed tasks to the right of "Today" were bona fide, completed work-aheads. The task managers provided details on the effort that had been expended to complete them and we totaled the amount. The total was not enough to balance out the late tasks.

With the red string focusing attention on the detailed status as of "Today" we could all see that we were beginning to fall behind. and would have to do our best to catch up.

What Happened Next

The contractors' game of just saying, "We're doing fine," was over. They had been playing a game of "Chicken". They had kept their progress reporting purposely vague while they waited to see if someone else would report a slip. If someone else did report a slip they could then admit to their own slip and claim that they were being held up by the other slippage. Now, they had to admit their slippages up front.

We moved the line each day and discovered that, in addition to its ability to stop the game-playing with the progress reporting, it also provided new and compelling motivation to the task leaders for those whose lagging tasks were now so obviously apparent to the left of "Today". Another bonus was the opportunity for us to recognize the task leaders who were ahead of schedule.

Wizard Comment

Now, for the first time, instead of dealing with a broad look at our progress we could all very clearly see the real lateness problem on a task-by-task basis and start to deal with our problems.

Before the application of the Today Line the task managers saw their tasks as 3-4 week chunks of an 18 month effort. For them, a day here or a day there was seen as insignificant in terms of the overall job. If they were a little behind here or there they would probably be able to take care of that by the end of the project.

The Today Line changed all that. It reminded them of their real task deadlines, some of which were right here and right now. They saw that being late today had to be addressed today – not at some future, unspecified time during the remaining months.

(Continued))

Wizard Comment

(Concluded)

We reminded them of the well-known answer that software guru Fred Brooks gave when asked how projects get to be several years late: “One day at a time”. We all agreed that there would be no more small slippages.

The Today Line is a standard feature in most current project management software programs. It is there to do just what our red string did, keep task mangers focused on the things they need to have done by today. You don’t need any fancy software for this. Just keep handy a good piece of red string.

Here again, in this tale, the key is remembering to focus tightly on the key data.

SEE HOW TO GET AND STAY ORGANIZED

SEE CHRIS ORGANIZE HIS PRESENTATION

SEE THE WORLD'S BEST PDA

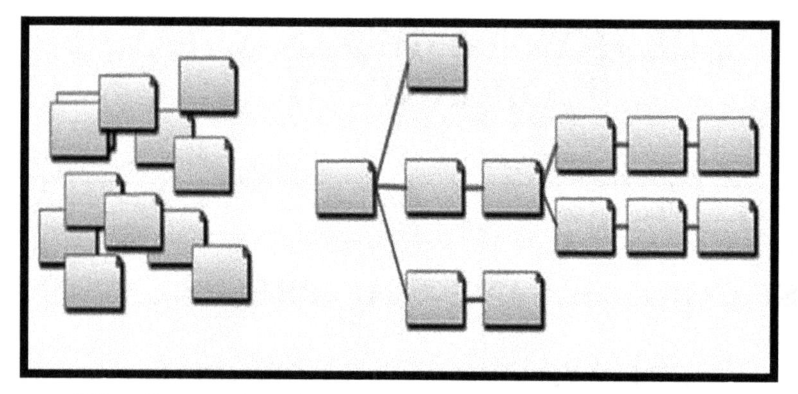

Un-Organized **Organized**

SEE HOW TO GET AND STAY ORGANIZED

A Bit of History

Imagine having an electronic device that would replace your human personal assistant – something that would get you organized and keep you organized throughout your busy days. To get you organized, your assistant would take all your incoming information and arrange it according to your personal way of thinking in neat, easily accessible files where you (or the assistant) could easily access it as needed. Then, as part of keeping you organized, your assistant would start your day with a cheery, "Good morning, Professor Jones. Today you have a faculty meeting at ten and office hours from 11:00 to noon. And this afternoon you are teaching from 2:00 to 3:45. The Assistant would describe your day so that you could see and get what you had to do.

A few years ago the folks in Silicon Valley figured they could develop an electronic assistant. They developed several devices called Personal Data Assistants (PDA). These are a class of pocket electronic devices that include specialized applications to store and retrieve, phone numbers, addresses, To-Do lists, and calendars. These devices also communicate and synchronize with computers and the internet.

The designers wanted these devices to maintain in one place all the data someone would need to know about one's daily activities and make it available as needed. The devices they created were intended to be used by people who could navigate quickly among the various applications to obtain the data as needed. Several different brands were developed and BlackBerry© became the leader of the pack.

However, as is true with many great electronic ideas, the electronics worked well but the overall capability never approached the performance of a human personal assistant. At best, one could quickly get all the required data but there was no way to integrate all of that into an easily visualized picture of what would be happening today.

The functions of the PDAs have now been inherited by Apple and Android smartphones where they exist along with many other applications. However, the applications are still not integrated in a way that facilitates the user's visualization of the events and activities of the day. They still fall far short of the original goal of matching or exceeding the capabilities of the human personal assistant. That is the situation that leads us to these tales.

Two Different Ways to Organize

The tales in this section illustrate the two "personal assistant" modes for organizing, maintaining and presenting information to help users see the content in a useful way. It's about how they ensure WYSIWYG.

Chris's Tale

The first tale is about Chris and how he tried a variety of modern data visualization assistants until he found one that suited the way he sees. Although Chris's tale relates a one-time event it is the type of thing he does often, frequently using a variety of the currently available organizing tools in combination.

Data visualization tools, often called "Mind Mapping" provide useful ways to brainstorm, make a plan, or turn ideas into the steps needed to make it real. Read this from the description of one of the software tools:

> *Product X is extremely flexible, works great on any desktop OS, and makes it easy to organize your ideas and thoughts in a variety of different styles, diagrams, and designs. You can use simple mind maps if you choose, or "fishbone" style flowcharts if you prefer. You can even add images and icons to differentiate parts of a project or specific ideas, add links and multimedia to each item, and more. If you're a project manager, you can even use Product X's built-in Gantt view to manage tasks in a way your colleagues may be familiar with.*

Chris has mastered several of the tools and his tale will illustrate how he used one of them.

Bob's Tale

The second tale starts out with Bob who is a very busy guy. It's about how he accomplishes the "staying organized" part of the personal assistant's job. Bob's work is fast paced and constantly changing.

Bob's tale is about seeing as a continuous process in the face of constant change. Bob has a type of PDA that is different and is not likely to be replaced by smartphone applications very soon. There are lots of surprises in Bob's tale so be sure to keep going to the end. There are actually three parts to Bob's tale, each one with a surprise for you.

SEE CHRIS ORGANIZE A PRESENTATION

What Shall I Say

The Program Director of the local Project Management Institute Chapter asked Chris if he could develop a one-day course in Leadership. She knew that Chris had lots of experience as a successful leader and project manager and was sure that he would have a lot to say about the leadership aspects of project management that the Chapter members would find interesting and enlightening.

Chris accepted. Then he began to get a bit concerned. He did have lots of experience and a lot of published material on leadership. His concern was that there was so much material. He couldn't see how to organize all of that into an outline for the course. He talked with a couple of his colleagues and they suggested that he consider trying some of the on-line visualization tools. These tools have different ways of sorting through large piles of data and presenting it in different ways. Perhaps one of them would take what he had and would help him see a coherent pattern in the data that would help him get an understanding of how he could organize his outline and his course materials.

Starting Out

Chris had seen one of his colleagues use an on-line tool called Wordle to create a summary of an e-book that he had written. That tool takes blocks of text of any size, sorts and counts all the words, drops common prepositions and conjunctions, and prepares a visual display of the words with the words scaled to size in relation to their frequency.

Chris had a number of technical papers on leadership that he thought would be a good set to use as a basis for the course so he copied all the text of those into a single block, gave it to Wordle and hit Go.

Chris's Wordle Output

That didn't help Chris.

Other Products

Chris looked at several other visualization tools that mine and organize the words or data in different ways. Most of these are free.

Then he tried a product called Mind Map. That works by letting the user (one or many) freely associate words that come to mind and then prepare a picture of the associations.

- MindMeister
- MindManager
- XMind
- FreeMind
- iMindMap
- SpiderScribe
- Coggle
- Freemind
- Text2MindMap
- Popplet
- Bubbl.us
- Mind42

Mind Map Output

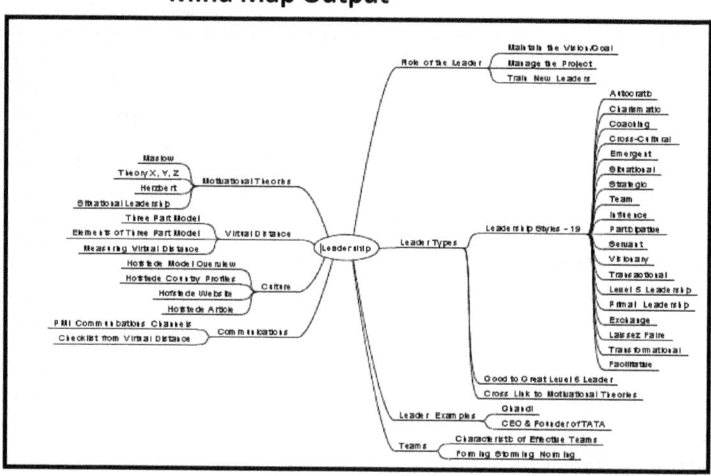

Chris found the Mind Map display really "spoke to him". Looking at it he could see a good way to organize the material he had. He went ahead and prepared the outline for the course.

Concept Map Origin

According to Grayson H. Walker at The University of Tennessee at Chattanooga: "Concept maps have their origin in the learning movement called constructivism. In particular, constructivists hold that prior knowledge is used as a framework to learn new knowledge. In essence, how we think influences how and what we learn. Concept maps identify the way we think, the way we see relationships between knowledge". Thus, mind maps are a valuable WYSIWYG tool – they help us see what we think.

Organizing in 3-D

Some of the projects Chris has managed involve development of information systems with very complex interactions among the various components. The picture shows a 3-D presentation of a concept mapping done with a product that can be used for visualizing a system of systems and the way they interact.

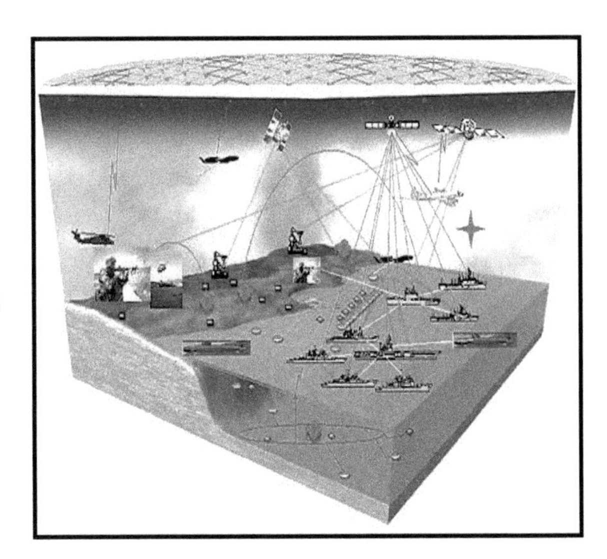

Wizard Comment

Chris tried a number of visualization tools and finally found one that matched his way of thinking and working. Using the tool helped him see the relative importance and the relationships among the many possible topics.

When he could see the relationships he got insights and a better understanding of how he could organize his presentation. He also found other, similar tools that might help him in other assignments.

There are new tools being developed every day. The lesson of Chris's tale is to find and use those that help you see what and how you think.

Intelligence is the ability to take in information from the world and to find patterns in that information that allow you to organize your perceptions and understand the external world.

-- Brian Greene

SEE THE WORLD'S BEST PDA

Part I - Modern Smart Phone Apps

The Wizard was with a friend and we were comparing the features of our new smart phones and trying to out-brag each other about all the helpful features we had on our phones. Hers had some really neat calendar and scheduling apps that she thought were really useful. My favorite new feature was the ability to input and store notes with voice entry. At one point we talked about problems with battery life. Neither of us could get through a full day of active use without plugging in somewhere. That's when my friend laughed and told me about Bob.

My friend said I really had to meet her colleague, Bob, and ask him about his marvelous **Battery Free PDA** (BFPDA). She told me that Bob is an "experienced" guy who has been working in the information systems world for a long time. In his work, Bob has specialized in the business of making systems user-friendly. He is not impressed with a lot of the new technology that looks like it is supposed to do wonderful things but really is hard to use and delivers very little for all the effort it requires. He is very, very practical. He favors things that are easy to use, are reliable, and do useful things efficiently.

She went on to say that Bob is a very early digital-native having worked with computers since IBM was a pup and computer guys wore white shirts and ties and had pocket protectors with five different color pens inside. The industry and Bob have come a long way since. Bob has kept up with things. He now wears sport shirts with no tie, has ditched the pocket protector, and is down to one pen and one pencil.

Battery Free Personal Data Assistant (PDA)

She said that Bob has, and uses a smartphone for e-mail and texting and lots of other things but he uses what he calls his "Battery Free PDA" to plan for and keep track of the things he has to do. He developed the concept in his early working years and has been using and refining it since then and he claims that no single app or combination of apps on current PDAs or smartphones can do it better for him.

With all of the technology and apps available today it's hard to believe that Bob could have something that would be better. My friend said, "Wait until you see what that is and why he uses it".

This was too amazing to believe. It sounded even more exciting than Google glasses and some of the other recent inventions. I figured I really had to meet with Bob and find out more. I really wanted to learn: how he uses it; why he thinks it's better than conventional PDAs and; how it can possibly do all the things my friend mentioned without batteries. Most of all, I wanted to see it and find out the secret. How can it possibly work without batteries?

Talking with Bob

After I tracked down Bob we had a chance to talk about his invention. It turned out that my friend had described him well. In recent years he has been consulting and teaching and is very familiar with the current devices and apps that are available. He is very practical minded and is always looking for the easiest and most effective ways to do whatever he has to do.

Bob does not use the organizer apps on his smartphone phone. He has found those to be quite inefficient, too cumbersome to learn and use. He does use some of the other phone apps for things that they do best (e.g., phone, e-mail, lookup, map and travel info). He has integrated the use of those apps with the BFPDA in a seamless way.

How Bob Uses His BFPDA

Bob was happy to tell me about the many ways he uses his BFPDA to organize his days. He uses it to record all the tasks he wants to accomplish each day, meetings he needs to attend, keep track of where he has to go, calls he has to make, any ideas that happen to pop into his head, and special notes to himself. Everything he needs to know about his day is visible, in one place, all the time. It helps him see everything that he has to be concerned with each day in a way that makes it easiest for him to understand (get) what he has to be doing as the day progresses. What he sees on the BFPDA is what he "gets" about his actions for the day.

Remarkably, as implied by its name, the BFPDA is completely battery-free. It uses no electricity and so it never needs to be charged. Bob doesn't have to worry about battery levels, carry a charger, or worry about where he can find an outlet for charging. It can be operated anywhere even in place with no electricity within miles. It's great for people traveling in remote areas. No hot spot required to operate. The BFPDA is always ready.

BFPDA vs. PDA

Bob really enjoyed telling me about the many ways that the BFPDA is better for him than the current crop of PDAs and their related apps on smartphones. He described the key features in several categories.

Data Entry

All data entry is manual. The BFPDA surface is rugged. Data entry can be made with a pen, pencil, marker, or even a crayon if nothing else is available. The data entry method is particularly good for Bob. Bob did not grow up using a keyboard, especially one as small as the one that pops up on his smartphone. Pencils work just fine for him and he always has one handy.

Bob said that he is not a good texter. Current PDA keys are too small for him and his aim isn't that great. Let's just say that those keyboards are meant for younger people, not for seniors. He pities the digital natives of today who will grow old with calluses on their thumbs.

He bragged that there is no limit on the amount of data that can be entered and no carrier data plan charges for any amount of storage. Additional storage is readily available if needed and is very inexpensive.

Technical Reasons – Lots of them.

All of the data on the BFPDA is always available at a moment's notice. No need to tap an app icon or press a button. There is no wait time for an app to fire up.

- Backup is automatic. The original is preserved and must be manually erased to get rid of it.
- Yes, you can lose it or drop it in water but your chances of recovery are sure a lot better than if you did the same with a conventional PDA
- Nobody is likely to steal the BFPDA. How about your PDA?
- If the BFPDA does get stolen the thief doesn't get your whole life history and personal data.

- Nobody can trace your whereabouts or mine data the BFPDA electronically.
- It can be used in areas where highly classified work is being done and electronic devices are prohibited.
- You never have to shut off the BFPDA during a meeting. In fact, you can use it during meetings and even refer to it during the performance of a show or movie without disturbing others.

But let's look at some of the other reasons Bob like the BFPDA. You may be surprised to learn about them.

Personal Reasons

- **Nothing Extraneous** - The "picture" of the day is never cluttered up by all your e-mails and internet "stuff"
- **No Temptation to Waste Time** - When you are using the BFPDA there is no temptation to check your e-mail of surf for news or any of the other time wasters that PDAs lure you into. It protects you from being drawn into those time-wasting activities.

At Last – The Secret is Revealed

While reading all about this wonderful invention you have likely been wondering how it could possibly work. At last, we can reveal the secret way that Bob has found to apply the WYSIWYG principles in the way that is most useful to him.

Bob's BFPDA is a set of 3 x 5 note cards that he keeps in his shirt pocket along with his smartphone in the place where Bob's vinyl pocket protector used to reside in the early days. Bob keeps and maintains his list of pending tasks on the cards. At the top of the deck is the "Today" card. It lists all of the tasks that he wants to accomplish today.

Everything on the card is handwritten or drawn. Bob puts a line at the top and above that writes the Day (e.g., Wednesday). Below the line under the Day Bob writes a note to remind him of each task that he will try to finish today. These notes are not detailed descriptions; they are words or phrases that remind Bob of each task.

Bob puts a line down the right hand side of the card and to the right of that he lists the places he has planned to go to during the day (e.g., Doctor, Bank, office supply store).

By looking at the Today Card, Bob can instantly see a complete picture of where he has to go and what he expects to accomplish today.

As the day progresses and Bob goes places and does things he strikes out the items on the card to show that they have been done. He also adds new items as they come up. Sometimes he may add a special note, e-mail address or a phone number of someone he needs to get in touch with later, maybe tomorrow.

Bob follows a disciplined Today Card maintenance process. At the end of the day, Bob checks to see what he has completed. (Think: "Sense of Satisfaction or Disappointment"). He creates a Today Card for the next day and carries over anything that he still needs to do. He then adds any new things that he will need to try to get done on that day. His last step is to retire the current Today Card by striking through it to show that everything on it has been properly addressed – either done or carried over or now not needed. That card goes to the back of the pack where it will sit until Bob remembers to put it on his stack of completed cards in a box next to his computer at home.

Why Does Bob Do It This Way?

Bob's smartphone has apps that do all of these things: task lists; schedules; travel, and more. Why doesn't he use those? There are lots of reasons but the biggest one is that this method provides him with the best way for him to see what he needs to do and get (understand and stay focused on) the full picture of each day.

And, finally, the cards work for Bob. They perfectly suit his way of seeing what he needs to do each day in a way that he can fully understand how he needs to organize and attack all the tasks at hand.

His Battery Free PDA is his WYSIWYG tool. What he "sees" on his cards, he "gets".

Keep Going! There's a big surprise in Part II ---- >

Part II - Hard to Believe, But True

In 2004, a San Francisco blogger, Mike Mann, authored a tongue-in cheek article in his blog about a marvelous new invention, the Hipster PDA (hPDA). Mann's article was intended to take a poke at the increasing expense and complexity of personal digital assistants. Mann thought up a catchy name for his new organizer, generated some technical sounding marketing language and posted a write-up at his ***Web log, 43folders.com***, a site where he meditates on Mac-related products and shares productivity tips.

Does this sound familiar?

Mann described the hPDA as "a fully extensible system for coordinating incoming and outgoing data for any aspect of your life and work". The hPDA that Mann described was a pack of 3x5 cards held together with a binder clip.

(Wizard note: Bob never heard about the article until recently.)

In a 2005 interview with The Washington Post, Mann said, "Consumers have been trained to instinctively believe that technology can solve all a person's problems -- that a trip to the electronics store is all that stands between a person and organization". Mann added, "The hPDA concept is a matter of using the right tool for the job and a philosophical decision about the kind of technology to let into your life".

He concluded the interview with this comment: "The number of gadgets folks lug around is creeping ever upward, but do you really need to carry $1,000 worth of equipment to have coffee with friends and be able to write down what albums you should check out?"

Following widespread coverage in the media and blogs, a lot of younger techies thought it might work for them. The idea went viral. Since then it has been accepted warmly by many and has become a popular personal management tool particularly with followers of David Allen's Getting Things Done methodology.

The hPDA Today

The slightly tongue-in-cheek blog entry seems to have clicked with his readers. At Flickr.com, a Web site where bloggers collectively gather and share pictures of whatever they're into now, there are almost 200 photos of hPDAs in use, made by users around the world. Odder still, the folks using these homemade organizers are no Luddites; in many of the shots, laptops, fancy cell phones and digital cameras clamor for space alongside the index cards.

It's Now a Huge Business

Although it began as a joke, or perhaps a statement about technology fetishism, the hPDA has rapidly gained popularity with serious users. Many are exchanging tips on Internet mailing lists. Advocates of the hPDA claim that it is a cheap, lightweight, freeform organizer that doesn't need batteries and is unlikely to be stolen.

It has also become a huge business opportunity. There are sites that sell hPDA card cases and special card clips. Enthusiasts also design and share index-card-size printable templates for storing contacts, to-do lists, calendars, notes, project plans, and so on. A product called the Hipster Nano PDA utilizes business cards with blank backs and one that has a calendar on the back. And so it continues.

Epilogue:

Bob and a lot of his fellow engineers and project managers were using their early versions of the hPDA to help keep their days organized long before Mann and his article. Most of them still do.

...and they never have to buy batteries or use a charger.

Keep going! There's another surprise in Part III.

FLASH – Just Announced

New Product Announcement

Adhesive notes for iPhone. We know what you're thinking -- there are apps for that. Well, it's still easier to jot something down on a sticky note, and more satisfying to cross off an item with real ink. With Paperback, you can do a quick sketch or make a list the old-fashioned way, and slap it on the back of your phone.

Use them one at a time, or put a small stack on the back of your phone to use later. Paperback's pages have a removable adhesive on most of their surface, keeping the note flat on your iPhone.

Designed for use with iPhone 5, 5s, and 5c. 80 sheets per pad.

Wizard Comment

Maybe Bob has always been way ahead of his time with his BFPDA. New technology can be great but sometimes the "old way" is the best way for some folks to see what they do. Everyone sees differently.

Let's have some respect for the tried and true methods.

TWO MORE WAYS TO SEE

SEE IKIWISI MEET WYSIWYG

SEE AND LEARN IN 3-D

Everyone has a photographic memory; some just don't have film.

Steven Wright

TWO MORE WAYS TO SEE

What You See and How You See It

Up to this point you have read about many different ways the Wizard has been involved in helping others achieve a WYSIWYG experience. There are many more ways but the next two tales were probably the most difficult. They are good indicators of how much effort and ingenuity may be required to achieve WYSIWYG.

See IKIWISI Meet WYSIWYG

Successfully specifying system requirements in advance is difficult. But when individual users or group-interactive systems are involved, it proves nearly impossible. Users asked to specify requirements in advance of development generally claim, "I don't know how to tell you, but **I'll know it when I see it".** The acronym for that is IKIWISI. Many users initially feel that they will only "know it" (i.e., get or understand it) when they see a demo or prototype.

Users' needs and desires change once the users work with the demonstration versions or begin operating the system and gain a deeper understanding of how it could support their mission. Thus, new requirements tend to emerge with continued use and mission understanding rather than be pre-specified.

The process for dealing with an IKIWISI client may involve use of many different methods to enable the client to understand their true needs more clearly and see how the emerging product will meet those needs. Client satisfaction depends on your ability to work effectively with the client through the IKISWISI process to the point where you and the client are in complete agreement. Then you can assure your client that what they see is what they will get -- and they will love it.

See and Learn in 3-D

Spatial ability and spatial skills in the general population vary widely. They have been significant areas of research in educational psychology since the 1920s or 1930s. Spatial visualization is the mental manipulation of spatial information to determine how a given spatial configuration would appear if portions of that configuration were to be rotated, folded, repositioned, or otherwise transformed.

In the second tale in this section the Wizard will describe a particularly difficult spatial visualization problem and how it was solved. There is an interesting twist to this tale. You will see how the visualization problem that stumped the engineers was solved by someone with no engineering training but lots of visualization skill.

Visual Thinking

Visual thinking helps us by giving us a way to see problems not as an endless variety of things that go wrong, but as a small set of interconnected visual challenges, each one of which can be pictured more clearly on its own.

Dan Roam in *The Back of the Napkin*

WYSIWYG

SEE IKIWISI MEET WYSIWYG

Refurbishing a Visual Treasure

Some years ago the Wizard had the privilege of being selected to be the project manager of a project to refurbish and re-equip the Assembly Chamber in the New York State Capitol building in Albany, New York. The job included many technical, political, and other challenges.

Known as the "People's Chamber," the home of the New York State Assembly is an historical and architectural treasure. Designed in a Moorish-Gothic style – a trademark of its renowned American architect, Leopold Eidlitz, it was dedicated on January 1, 1879 to national acclaim. It is the largest room in the New York State Capitol, the first of the distinctive building's "Grand Spaces". In 1888, it was the first public room in the capitol and the first in the nation to be lit with electric lights.

The job was to design, build and install new state-of-the-art lighting, sound reinforcement, paging, and electronic voting systems. Along with that, it required replacing the chamber carpet and cleaning and refurbishing all visible features including decorative stone friezes and statuary.

The work began the day after the end of the Assembly session at the end of March and had to be finished completely by January 4 when the governor would be coming to the Assembly to present the traditional State-of-the-State address. The deadline was absolute. Missing the deadline was politically unacceptable.

Counsel for the Majority – The Top Manager

The person who was in charge of the project was a lawyer whose official title was Counsel to the Majority. He was the chief decision-maker and he held the purse strings for the job. He had no background in construction or any of the other specialties involved in the work. He was politically savvy and concerned about appearances – how the chamber and its new equipment would look when we were finished.

The Project Team

The contractor team included 11 different specialties, (e.g., construction, lighting, sound, interior design). The contractor leads met at the end of each day to resolve issues and set the course for the next day. A special feature of that meeting was the review and discussion of progress photos taken during the day.

The IKIWISI Part

In meetings with the Counsel to the Majority, as various contractors were trying to explain what they were planning to do or build, the Counsel would try to see what they were talking about but usually could not. When that occurred, he would say, "I'll Know It When I See It". In response to that we developed a strategy that involved artist renderings, physical models, and demonstrations.

As we conceived and designed new equipment and installations, we would first have an artist draw a picture of what it would look like when installed. If the Counsel liked that, we would go to the next step and build a physical mock-up of the item. Then, after approval by the Counsel, we would produce and install the final product. In each of these steps we tried to make sure that what we were showing was as close as possible to the final in appearance.

Member Desk Rendering

Equipment Mock Up

Final Product

Voting Display Mock Up

Display Rendering

Final Version

The WYSIWYG Part

The IKIWISI process worked well. Sometimes, a few iterations of the renderings or models were required but the end product, a fully satisfied client, was worth the extra effort.

Photo Coverage

Several of the contractors carried and used their cameras to capture pictures of problems and progress on their parts of the project. Review of the photos was on the agenda for every morning team meeting. The photos were an indispensable visualization tool for this job.

Photos helped see the unseen. The camera saw it all. The team members all had many distractions while working but the cameras did not. The cameras saw everything and remembered it. Taking photos from the same spots each day allowed the team to see the rate of progress of the demolition and construction in a time-lapse view. They could see what they were getting done.

Wizard Comment

The combination of renderings, models and photos was absolutely vital in helping the client and the team see how the requirements were evolving. That was IKIWISI for the client and WYSIWYG for both the client and the team.

Photos provided a solid record that allowed all the team members to see the same view of what was happening and provided the basis for discussions required to resolve many of the issues. That was WYSIWYG for the team

At the end of the project, the renderings, models and the photos helped show off what had been done. The photos showing before and after views told a great story. They helped the citizens of New York State see what they had gotten for the money they spent on the project. That was WYSIWYG for the New York taxpayers.

SEE AND LEARN IN 3-D

A Difficult Concept to Teach

The Wizard was working as an instructor in teaching mid-level managers the principles and best practices of Project Management and Systems Engineering. The textbook for the course was Visualizing Project Management and the basics of the course were well documented but complex and hard to teach. There were five interrelated aspects and the students had trouble seeing how all the relationships worked together throughout the project life cycle. A physical model of the process turned out to be the key teaching tool that made it easy for the students to see and understand the dynamics and the interplay of all the parts. The story of the development of the model is instructive.

Seeing Just With Words

Below is the description of the components of the concept. This is what the students had to read and try to understand.

As presented in the written description

There are five Essential aspects of project management concept that come into play during the project cycle. They are:

- Common Vocabulary
- Teamwork
- Project Cycle
- Project Management Elements
- Commitment

Common Vocabulary - The words used and understood by all participants on a project, tailored to the specific industry and project environment.

Teamwork – Working together to achieve a common goal – concurrent and timely involvement of project stakeholders, suppliers, operators, and maintenance experts

Project Cycle – The sequence of events jointly pursued by all project participants to achieve the common project goal – tailored to the type, phases, scope, and risk of the project.

10 Project Management Elements – The project management techniques and tools, grouped by use, into ten categories – situationally applied by the team to manage the project throughout the project cycle.

- Project Requirements
- Organization Options
- Project Team
- Project Planning
- Opportunity and Risk
- Project Control
- Project Visibility
- Project Status
- Corrective Action
- Project Leadership

Commitment – Commitment to success by management and all stakeholders throughout the life of the project.

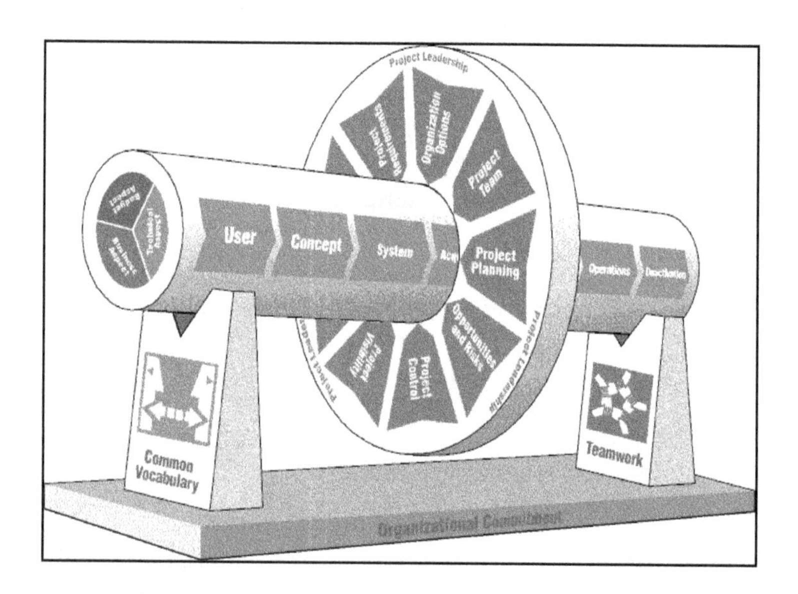

CSM Orthogonal Model ©

– (With Permission from Kevin Forsberg)

How the Orthogonal Model Came to Be Developed

While the concept was in its early stages and was still being described in words only the instructors frequently voiced their concerns about the difficulties in explaining it. Hard to see how it all works? You're not alone. Most students can't "see it" and "get it" from the words alone.

Hearing the complaints, one of the staff members in the unit that produced the teaching materials came up with a way to show all the interactions in a simple, physical model. She put together a demonstration prototype using a paper towel tube and some other pieces and presented it for consideration. Her visualization model worked. The picture shows what it looks like and how the Essentials were represented.

Helping Students See How it Works

Three of the components are relatively static. Common Vocabulary, Teamwork, and Commitment must be present throughout the life of a project.

Commitment is shown as the base, ultimate foundation for the whole process.

Common Vocabulary and Teamwork are key supporting components. They are the legs supporting the active parts of the model.

The Project Cycle, from start to finish, is depicted along the side of the tube. The tube includes all of the steps from project start to end. The Project Management Elements are in play at every stage of the project cycle and must be performed as the situation dictates at each stage.

The 10 Project Management Elements are shown on the disk. To show that any of these may come into play at any time throughout the project cycle, the disc can slide from one end of tube (project start) to the other (project end).

Wizard Comment

If a picture is worth a thousand words a physical model of a complex, dynamic process with parts that move in tune with the process is probably worth ten times that when you are trying to help others see how the process works.

Potholes and bumps? Welcome to the world. Every road has them. They're there to be navigated, avoided, driven over, or through to the other side.

Don't keep driving into the pothole.

-- Nora Roberts

SEE POTHOLES ON THE PATH TO WYSIWYG

SEE DEMONSTRATION POTHOLES

SEE ACRONYM POTHOLES

SEE VISUAL POTHOLES

Regardless of the brilliance of your analysis or the importance of your insights, you need to be able to communicate your findings successfully to others. If you're the only one who "gets it," then you've failed. You need to consider how you can simplify your message so that it resonates with your audience and they know how to act on your insights.

If your analysis findings aren't capturing your audience's attention, you either have the wrong numbers or the wrong audience. In other words, you've either failed to understand what's important to your audience or you've failed to identify the right audience who would care about your findings.

-- Brent Dykes, author of Web Analytics Action Hero

SEE POTHOLES ON THE PATH TO WYSIWYG

The tales you have read show some of the different ways the Wizard has been able to help individuals and groups make their way along the path to WYSIWYG. Those you have read about have learned how to see clearly and get (i.e., understand) completely and act confidently to improve what they do. These are the WYSIWYG success stories and they are examples that show ways that you might be able to use in your own activities.

However, there are other tales and these are about where, either intentionally or accidentally, WYSIWYG doesn't happen. There are many things that can inhibit WYSIWYG and we call them "Potholes on the Path to WYSIWYG".

Intentional Potholes

Unfortunately, there are some people who may have a vested interest in keeping you from seeing clearly what is going on. They want to make sure that you do not experience true WYSIWYG.

Lying is one approach. There are many guides published on "How to Lie With _____". They show many of the ways that slides, statistics, and other items can be presented in ways that are misleading. (Example: A politician describing his opponent states that in the last election he ran "Next to last" without mentioning that it was a two person race.) These books are not meant to encourage lying, rather, they are intended to point out the potholes on your way to WYSIWYG that you should try to avoid.

Some other kinds of potholes to watch out for include the favorites of those who have to present bad news and would like to keep the worst parts hidden. Their techniques include selective omission of details, euphemisms, and obfuscation. (The Wizard should also mention the use of unfamiliar words such as euphemism and obfuscation to confuse folks.)

Magicians don't want their audiences to see how they saw the lady in half or produce the rabbit out of the hat so they use misdirection to trick people into not seeing what they are getting. This type of pothole is not limited to magicians. Politicians can keep you from seeing their favorable vote on something you don't like by focusing your attention during the voting on some other issue.

In his book, *Nudge*, Richard Thaler describes a very common pothole based on exploiting human inertia, the tendency to keep doing what we have always been doing. He points out that most people fail to pay attention and thus don't see that a contract that you signed has an automatic renewal clause that will continue a monthly charge past the anniversary date forever unless you take action to stop it. Let's add default clauses to the list of potholes.

Although there are many more types of intentional potholes we will end with this example:

STANDARD DISCLAIMER: Please read all instructions and warnings before use. Must be 18 years of age or older to proceed further. Enter at your own risk. Some assembly required. Batteries not included. You are responsible for all errors, even those made by the author. Always read the fine print.

Accidental Potholes

The accidental potholes on the way to seeing are those that nature creates for us. They are the imperfections and idiosyncrasies of the world in which we live and work. These are the potholes that we have to look out for and be prepared to avoid.

There are several types of media that we can use to try to help ourselves and others see. We can:

- Write something
- Say something (e.g., speech, briefing)
- Show one or more pictures
- Give a demonstration (e.g., an activity, a device, a combination)

When We Write or Say Something

There are many ways in which a person trying to read the written word can feel like what he or she is reading is in a foreign language. The wording may be too complex. The words may be unfamiliar.

Some may have a limited vocabulary and all the words beyond those that they know are, to them, a foreign language.

- There may be regional differences in the terminology (e.g. is a poke a bag or a sock or a punch?).
- In areas where the pace of life is leisurely and you ask when something will be done, "shortly' may turn out to be days or weeks.
- Those who see the words but are not able to make any sense out of them can't see and do not get anything out of the situation except frustration.
- Variations in the English language and extensive use of idioms increase the problem. Does everyone know what is meant by "That dog won't hunt"?

Problems with Spoken Words

Many of the seeing problems with the written word are made worse when the words are being spoken. Some people do not hear clearly. When you are speaking to them they may mis-hear some of the words and that will lead to a confused message. Some do not hear and process spoken words quickly. Fast speakers are often misunderstood by such people. The translation process can get really stressed when you are speaking quickly and what you are saying is full of jargon and acronyms.

Sarcasm

It depends on your tone of voice but your listeners may think you are being sarcastic when you say, "That was really **great**!". Was it something that your group had done that was really good or something really bad?.

Different Frames of Reference

The optimist sees the glass as half full. The pessimist sees it as half empty. The engineer sees that the glass is the wrong size.

Frame of Reference

Someone watching you demonstrate some new cost-saving technology may end up thinking about the poor people who will be losing jobs because of it.

Ambiguity (Context and vocal stress)

The meaning of the following sentence changes radically depending on which word is emphasized.

I think I see a moving van

Do you see a family van with a Mom driving the kids to school that is moving? ... or do you see one of those big trucks in carrying furniture, moving or not? Also,, do you really see it? ... or do you just think you see it?

Misdirection

Sometimes the words can lead you into a mental trap by misdirection. For example, answer this question: A big elephant and a small elephant are walking together in the circus parade. The little elephant is the big elephant's son. The big elephant is not the little elephant's father. Who is the big elephant?

The trick in this riddle is to catch you when your mind is preset to think that all big elephants are male. Mom elephants can be big also and you have to remind folks to remain open-minded in order to see better.

Believability

A quote from a recent report on a test of a communication link: "During testing there were only three instances of undetected error ..." Some might let that statement pass without thinking. An inquiring mind would require and answer to: "How did they find those undetected errors? *

* In this case, the testers explained they had inserted 100 errors into the test message and only 3 sneaked past the test. That explanation was necessary to make it possible to "**See**" how the test was done.

Jargon Problems

Jargon problems can be severe but are more easily overcome. Some work groups use acronyms and specialized jargon extensively. This is very prevalent in military and technical circles. Those who actively work in these groups, the "insiders" are thoroughly familiar with all the words and find it easy to process the acronyms and jargon as they read or hear them. To an outsider, some of the things that are written seem like a foreign language.

"Seeing" Problems with Pictures or Data

As you saw in Sarah's tale, some have difficulty visualizing the relationships among components of a related set of activities. When they read or are told about these activities they tend to see all the things going on as separate tasks and cannot picture the relationships among them.

In the tale about the Wizard and Ernie, you saw that some people can look at a spreadsheet full of data and "see" the story in the numbers. Others, whether they have math fright or some other aversion to numbers, may freeze up at a set of numbers and have to find a different way to see the story. (See books by Edward Tufte in the References). To facilitate WYSIWYG, you must be aware that what works for some may not work for others and be prepared to offer a variety of approaches.

Some people have never been trained to translate written descriptions of objects into a mental image of the object or activity. They can read a description of a new building or device but they cannot comprehend what it looks like from the words alone. To understand, they must see a physical model. (See IKIWISI Meets WYSIWYG)

You can adapt your presentation methods to most of these problems. They are the inherent characteristics of your intended audience and you must be aware that you will have to use special methods when you are working with people with these reading impairments. Work with persons who have reading or visualization problems. Talk with them about what you are trying to do to help them get to WYSIWYG.

In the tales that follow in this section you will see some more examples of the verbal or written potholes. These are some of the most common and the most difficult to avoid.

Technical Jargon

Problems with the Regurgitive Purwell -- Most of our errors are being caused by parastatic conductance resulting from the differential spurving of the hydroscopic marslevanes located in the prefabulated amilite base of the unilateral detractor mechanism. We have attempted to fix this by manestically spacing the grouting brushes on the periphery of the nubbing purwell but this has not been effective.

Madison Avenue "Mad Men" Jargon

The boss asked us to think out of the box so we pushed the envelope, took a helicopter view and decided to boil the ocean a bit. We put on our end user face and concluded that a land and expand approach would be a win-win for everybody. So, as soon as we get our ducks in a row we can move forward with the folks from the cubicle farm doing the heavy lifting but keeping us in the loop.

SEE DEMONSTRATION POTHOLES

Recommended Best Practices for Demonstrations

- Make sure the viewer sees significant benefit to be achieved (i.e., Consistent with the viewer's language and culture.
- Make it easy to try
- Make it easy to evaluate

Failure to achieve ANY of these impairs the ability of the attendees to see and get point of the demonstration.

The Demo No One Could See and Get

In February, 2008, the director of advertising for the Google-owned video service, YouTube, was unable to play a single one of her videos during her presentation. Her speech began with a jerky start while she waited for the introductory video to roll, but she gracefully ad-libbed with a recruiting pitch before giving up on that video.

Later she tried to highlight a video of an ad by Heinz as an example of viral advertising but it, too, failed to display on the big screens. She had to describe the video with words instead. Over and over, the videos sprinkled through her speech failed to appear on the screens.

"This is a little comical because this is YouTube and so far we've shown no videos," she said at one point. "It's also comical because this is now the technology industry association".

The system worked fine later, however, when local companies up for the awards were featured in short video clips. Of course, by then, the folks who were supposed to see it were no longer present.

Crash Demo Crashes

At a media event in Sweden, Volvo chose to demonstrate its latest technology: the new collision detection system on the S60. In this system, sensors in the car detect obstacles in the road ahead, applying the brakes to slow or even stop the car before a big crunchy mess occurs. A fine idea... so long as it works.

Volvo's engineers started up the car, pointed it at a truck, released the unmanned S60 from its hutch at a speed of just under 30 miles per hour, sat back and .... it smacked into the truck.

The collision detection system had worked perfectly several times before the crash. Volvo blamed the failure of the technology on a battery issue. They lamely claimed that this would have been easily spotted by a human driver.

What they hoped everyone would see was a state-of-the-art collision avoidance system. What the audience actually saw was the effectiveness of the S60's crash structures. Maybe it wasn't all bad.

Steve Jobs iPhone Demo at MacWorld 2007

In earlier demos of new Apple products Steve had experienced many problems so, for this one he took some extraordinary steps.

Steve opened by saying: "Every once in a while a revolutionary product comes along that changes everything". However, he knew that what he was about to demonstrate had lots of problems that could kill the effectiveness of the demo.

At the current stage of development the iPhone could play a section of a song or a video, but it couldn't play an entire clip reliably without crashing. It worked fine if you sent an e-mail and then surfed the Web. If you did those things in reverse, however, it might not. Hours of trial and error had helped the iPhone team develop what engineers called "the golden path," a specific set of tasks, performed in a specific way and order that made the phone look as if it worked.

Steve had AT&T, the iPhone's wireless carrier, bring in a portable cell tower, so they knew reception would be strong. Then, with Jobs's approval, they preprogrammed the phone's display to always show five bars of signal strength regardless of its true strength. Even with the special cell tower and a custom-built electronics lab backstage, the bugs persisted.

The iPhone's biggest problem was that it often ran out of memory and had to be restarted if made to do more than a handful of tasks at a time. Jobs had a number of demo units onstage with him to manage this problem. If memory ran low on one, he would switch to another while the first was restarted.

In 100 or so rehearsals, Jobs didn't make it through once without a glitch. Steve got through the demo and his Apple fans ignored the obvious fakery. The audience saw what they wanted to see, the promise of the new technology that, as Steve said, "...would change everything".

Wizard Comment

The rules for demos are no different from those for everything else – What you see is what you get. In the YouTube demo the audience didn't see what the presenter wanted to show. What they saw was an embarrassing failed attempt to claim technical excellence.

What they didn't see, they didn't get.

In the Volvo demo the audience did see a demo of the crash-worthiness of the car but the overall claim of technical superiority was seriously undermined.

What they saw made them get something else.

Jobs, once burned, was prepared for the worst. His extra phones, special communications lines, careful scripting, and rehearsals were key ingredients in his plan to make sure that his audience would see exactly what he wanted them to get.

What they saw was just what Steve wanted them to get.

Preparation pays off. We could all learn from that.

Acronym Jungle

SEE ACRONYM POTHOLES

Blinded By Lack of an AEM

At a recent meeting that included people from many different organizations the Wizard opened by having everyone introduce themselves to the group. He suggested that it would be best if people would not use acronyms in their introductions. As he explained, "I have left my AEM at home". He went on to say, "AEM stands for 'Acronym Expansion Module' and without that he would be unable to translate the acronyms you might use in your introductions".

What happened next was a real eye-opener. Most people had trouble remembering to spell out their organization or project name. Three were embarrassed by not knowing what their organization's acronym stood for.

The Chair's point was well made. Extensive use of acronyms can impede understanding. If the people who use the acronyms regularly have difficulty translating them, others certainly would.

Acronym Problems

Writing with lots of acronyms creates an alphabet soup. It guarantees that readers will remember nothing substantive and just how hard that was to read. This is most prevalent in military circles. This may derive from the fact that in the relatively recent past minimizing the number of characters in a communication was, in fact, an important element of telegraph-era warfare. Some writers not only accept, but embrace and positively *revel* in the military's acronym-happy culture. This helps mark them as "insiders" but it impairs WYSIWYG.

When the General Couldn't See It

An Army Major was trying to help his General see how the Joint Operations Planning and Execution System (JOPES) deals with logistics actions that are planned to occur before deployments. He was describing how the system handles it when the actual deployment dates have not yet been set. This is taken from the transcript of what he said:

"JOPES organizes the information obtained from the four databases, along with scenario-specific information, into a specific TPFDD plan known by a Plan Identification Number (PID). A PID directly corresponds to an OPLAN or CONPLAN and contains all of the unit line numbers and force modules (described below) associated with that plan's movement of forces. Dates associated with the movement of forces are known as C-days and N-days. A C-day is an unnamed day on which a deployment operation will commence. When used in conjunction with a C-day, an N-day indicates the number of days preceding the C-Day. For example, N–1 refers to 1 day before C-day, N–2 refers to 2 days before C-day, and so on. At execution of the deployment, an actual date is assigned as C-day".

Wizard Comment

For some reason the General didn't see it and didn't get it.

(The Wizard was with him at the time and he didn't get it either.)

WYSIWYG

SEE VISUAL POTHOLES

What You Don't See ...

According to the experts, retail spaces must be designed to draw people into the space to shop. The storefront must act as a billboard for the store. It should have large display windows that allow shoppers to see into the space and the product inside. Potential customers driving by should be able to get a sense of the wonderful shopping experiences that might be available inside. The following tales tell what happens when such advice is ignored.

A few miles away from where the Wizard lives are two examples of anti-WYSIWYG. These are situations where ***What You Don't See, You Don't Get***. These were both visualization disasters.

Rockville Mall – "Our Berlin Wall"

In 1972, as part of a long term urban renewal project, the town of Rockville, Maryland, opened a large new shopping mall with space for two major anchor stores, 40 shops and over 1,500 parking spaces. Within a year of the opening, the anchor store closed and was replaced by a succession of lesser retail operations. In 1979 the mall went bankrupt and was closed.

The mall was well situated at the intersection of two main highways but the facade that drivers could see from the most heavily travelled highway was bleak and forbidding. Locally, it was called "the Berlin Wall". It was a bland, two-story beige concrete bunker that scarcely resembled a mall to anyone who might drive past.

The view into the mall from the other street was not attractive. Aside from one distinctive entrance portal with a white peaked roof, fountains, and a mural there was nothing to indicate the possibility of a fine shopping experience.

What the Potential Patrons Saw

In 1983 the mall was redeveloped as a movie multiplex theater and connected to the newly opened Metro station. Though these businesses, at the east end of the mall closest to the Metro station, attracted some traffic, the remainder of the mall lacked attractive tenants and therefore remained largely vacant.

Later, the west end of the mall was finally torn down. The portion connected to the Metro station still exists as an office/health care/fitness center complex that is not recognizable as having once been part of a mall.

Mazza Gallerie – "Mammoth Marble Failure"

The Mazza Gallerie was built in 1978 as an upscale mall built to serve the population in the Bethesda - Chevy Chase, Maryland area at the northwest corner of the District of Columbia. Nieman Marcus was the initial anchor store and there were many other high-end shops.

The building was designed as a modernist box. There were few windows, small doors, and little presence on the street. The center did not live up to its potential, seeing high vacancy rates. In June 1997, a group that owned the Friendship Centre development across Wisconsin Avenue, acquired the center and embarked upon a major renovation.

The new design removed the knife-edged corner of the building and installed a three-story glass box and retail window, which faces a major gateway intersection at the border of Maryland and the District of Columbia. The design team created additional retail windows along the street; brightened and enlarged the Metrorail and Neiman Marcus entrances; and installed a series of sun shades and canopies that wrap the façade and create a pedestrian-scaled street.

At night, the canopy undersides are illuminated with programmable LED fixtures that create a dynamic beacon for pedestrians. Construction was completed in November 2006.

The redesigned Mazza Gallerie is very successful. The openings in the marble wall give shoppers who are passing by a glimpse of the delights inside.

Wizard Comment

WYSIWYG only works when you can see.

WYSIWYG

If You Don't Get It,
You Don't Get It

The Washington Post

If You Don't See It,
You Won't Get It

The Wizard

EPILOGUE

What You Have Seen

We have come to the tail end of this set of the WYSIWYG tales. In these tales you tales have seen some examples of how you can use simple visualization tools and techniques to:

- See and understand how things work
- See ways to solve problems
- See and improve coordination among teams
- Help others see things they can or should do
- See how to organize thoughts and activities
- See things that are really important and attract attention to them

Tales and Tools

As stated in the beginning, there is "No Magic Required" for this type of wizardry. None of the tales required any fancy or expensive tools, extensive training or any significant investment of time. Let's review.

Flow Charts

Sarah, the Oak Ridge group and the ad agency all found that they could see and fix their problems using a flow chart approach. The chart creation process brought out things that people knew but had not shared before and also exposed gaps in the knowledge of the affected persons.

Exposing the Data

Anne and Fred both got to see time by writing it down. Anne couldn't see "snippets" of time in her head but, when she wrote out a schedule and tracked it, the "snippets' became visible. When the Fred Sked came off Fred's computer and was publicly posted, everybody could see that it wasn't Fred's problem and the problem got fixed.

The Gap Method

Ralph, Click-Fix, the Eyesore folks, and the donor seekers provided ways for people to see what they needed to see to take required actions.

Focus

Recall the project team that finally saw their problems when their attention was brought into focus with just a simple piece of string

And also recall the police who now can "Look less and see more", just as a result of focusing their effort.

Personal Tools

Chris used tools he found on the web that suited his way of thinking. It was not hard for him to find them or use them. And, of course, good old Bob and all the users of the hPDAs are doing fine with some of the simplest tools possible – 3x5 cards and pencils.

Models and Prototypes

Even the more sophisticated problems did not required sophisticated solutions. Drawings, renderings, prototypes, and physical models were all that were needed for the IKIWISI folks to see what they would be getting.

Potholes

The tales have also reminded us of some of the impediments to clear seeing:

- How jargon, acronyms, and other language problems can hinder seeing
- How critical the choice of presentation graphics can be to seeing
- How situations can set the stage for seeing– or not
- How demonstrations can go wrong – or right

The Future of WYSIWYG

New visualization tools and techniques are currently being developed at a rapid pace and the rate is likely to accelerate as more and more data becomes available over the internet. In a few years, the advanced visualization applications of today will be superseded by far better, much faster ways for seeing.

Remember the Basics

What will remain the same, however, will be the need to ensure adherence to the basic principles that have been reflected in these tales.

- Think about what you want to see and what you want others to get
- Find and focus on the right data
- Make sure the data are accurate
- Fill all the potholes

... and that should ensure that

What You See Is What You Get

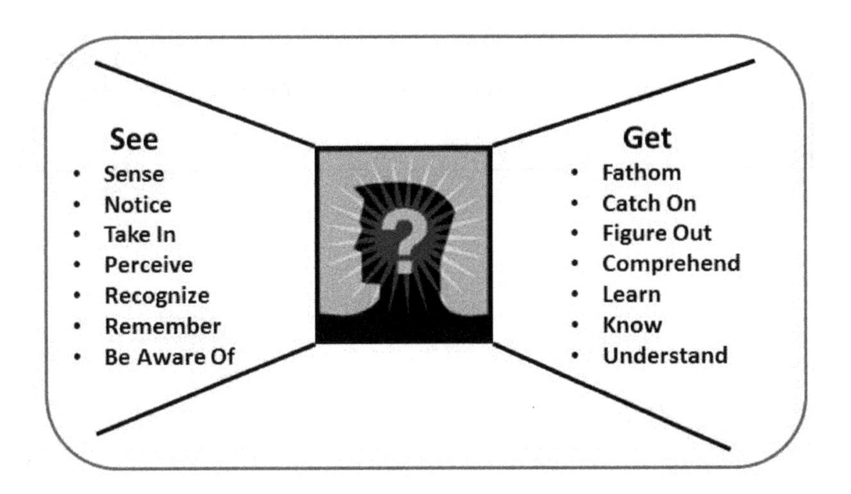

These are exciting times for information visualization, because we are still in the discovery phase, although this phase will not last for long. In the next few years, the wild inventions that are now being implemented will become standardized. Like clay sculptures that have been baked and hardened, the novel data visualization systems of today's laboratory will become cultural artifacts, everyday tools of the information professional.

Colin Ware
in *Information Visualization : Perception for design*

REFERENCES

WYSIWYG Beginnings

Almost Perfect, W. E. Pete Peterson, Prima Publishing; First Edition (June 1, 1994) 1998: **ISBN-10:** 0788199919, **ISBN-13:** 978-0788199912
A first-hand account of the problems involved in achieving WYSIWYG in a word processing program. Written by the creators of WordPerfect

Giant Brains;: Or, Machines that Think, Edmund Callis Berkeley, 1949
One of the earliest books to describe in detail the inner workings of digital computers. The author speculates that someday computers will do more than just manipulate data, they may think as humans do.

Seeing

Beautiful Evidence, Edward R. Tufte, Graphics Press; 1St Edition, July 2006, ISBN-10: 0961392177,ISBN-13: 978-0961392178

The Cognitive Style of PowerPoint: Pitching Out Corrupts Within, Second Edition [Paperback], Edward R. Tufte,

Envisioning Information: Edward R. Tufte, Graphics Press, Cheshire, CT, 1990, ISBN 0-9613921-1-8
A beautiful collection of cognitive art examples.

Information Graphics: A Comprehensive Illustrated Reference, Robert L. Harris, Management Graphics, Atlanta, GA, 1999, ISBN:0-19-513512-6
A comprehensive catalog of visualization methods.

Photography and the Art of Seeing: Freeman Patterson, Firefly Books, Ltd, Buffalo, NY, 2011, ISBN:*1554079802*
Careful descriptions of how good photographers see and how that helps them capture what others do not see.

Information Visualization: Perception for Design (Interactive Technologies), Colin Ware, 2012, Morgan Kaufmann,
ISBN-10: 0123814642 ISBN-13: 978-0123814647

Situations Matter: Understanding How Context Transforms Your World: Sam Sommers, Riverhead Books, NY, 2011, ISBN-10: 1594486204
Descriptions of how context and emotions shape what we see.

Visualizing Data, Ben Fry, O'Reilly Media, Inc., Sebastopol, CA, 2008, ISBN:10: 0-596-51455-7
A programmers' guide to methods for displaying data.

Visualizing Project Management (3rd ed.): Kevin Forsberg et.al., John Wiley & Sons, Hoboken NJ, 2005, ISBN: 978-0-471-64848-2
Presents a way to visualize the project management process.

Waiting

The Psychology of Waiting Lines: Donald A. Norman, Excerpt from Chapter 4, *Clerks and Waiting Lines*, from a draft book manuscript tentatively entitled *"Sociable Design,* 21 August 2008
One of the papers used by the protagonist as the basis for his work in the Commissary tale.

Plots of Conditional Wait-Time Intervals Provide Better Information to Queuing System Arrivals: Allen G. Greenwood, Published on-line in Decision Sciences, Volume 22 Issue 3, pages 473-483, 7 June 2007
One of the papers used by the protagonist as the basis for his work in the Commissary tale.

Presenting

Purpose, Movement, Color: A Strategy for Effective Presentations, Tom Mucciolo and Rich Mucciolo, Media Net, Inc. NY 1994, ISBN-10: 0964742802
Advice on how to create informative, useful charts.

The Back of the Napkin, Dan Roam, Digital Roam, 2008, ISBN: 978-1-59184-199-9
A collection of simple ways to present complex data and concepts to help others see what is important.

Project Management, Process Improvement

Continuous Process Improvement, Richard Y. Chang, Richard Y. Chang Associates, Irvine, CA, 1996, ISBN 1-883553-06-7
Describes ways to see opportunities for process improvement.

How to Lie With Statistics, Darrell Huff, W. W. Norton & Co., New York,1993, ISBN 0-393-31072-8
Describes many ways to present statistical data so that viewers see them the way you want to "spin" them – which may be truthful or not.

Seeing Action Opportunities

The Enjoyment of Management, Frederick C. Dyer, Dow Jones Irwin, Inc., Homewood, IL, 1971
A great book on management and the basis for the tales involving the Gap Method for stimulating action.

Nudge: Improving Decisions About Health, Wealth, and Happiness, Richard H. Thaler and Cass R. Sunstein, Yale University Press, New Haven, 2008, ISBN: 978-0-300-12223-7
A more recent presentation of the Gap Method

ABOUT THE AUTHOR

The WYSIWYG Wizard is an independent consultant specializing in process improvement and project management. Prior to his retirement he worked as a project manager with MITRE Corporation and SRA International developing and implementing major government information systems. At SRA he managed 85 projects with a perfect cost, schedule and performance record. Since retirement, he has taught project management and systems engineering for American University and the Center for Systems Management. At CSM he developed and ran a process improvement practice that has conducted over 100 process assessments.

Bill is currently working with GEMSOC LLC as a facilitator of process improvement workshops for government agencies and their contractors.

Other Publications by The Wizard

DrawWhatYouDo (e-book), Bill Flury, Smashwords.com, 2012,
ISBN: 9781301678013
This is the author's earlier book presenting one of the basic approaches to help individuals and work groups visualize and improve the things they do.

Forward Momentum Blog
http://forwardmomentum.net/motivating-process-improvement/

Where There's a Wall, There's a Way!, Bill Flury, 27 August 2012

Motivating Process Improvement, Bill Flury, January 11, 2013

SquawkPoint Blog
http://www.squawkpoint.com/2013/01/bestpractice-2

Good, Better, Best Practice, Bill Flury, January 2013

ACKNOWLEDGMENTS

Thanks to those who have helped me see different ways to see and improve what I do and have given me opportunities to help others to do the same.

At the Center for Systems Management , Kevin Forsberg, Hal Mooz, and Vanessa Binder and her daughter introduced me to the value of 3-D models in explaining complex project and process concepts. Mark Wilson, CEO at Strategy Bridge International, has been a continual supporter and has provided excellent opportunities to work WYSIWYG wizardry with his many and varied clients. The same is true of Deborah Hunt and Jeff Cummings at iPower, LLC, who have kept me active in formal process improvement activities.

Thanks also to Chris Fristad, CEO of GEMSOC, LLC, with whom I have worked for several years. We have worked together to develop the practical, no acronyms or jargon approach to project management and process improvement training that is reflected in this book.

Chris, Twyla Courtot, Diana Fraser, and Mary Flury have also helped me get through the publishing process with only the errors that I continue to make in spite of their careful reviews.

All of these people, the characters in the tales, and many more too numerous to mention have helped to shape the tales and I appreciate their contributions.

Special thanks to my colleague and long-time friend, Rick Gibson. Since we first met we have shared ideas and experiences in process improvement activities. Rick and I have worked together in many of the situations reflected in the tales. He has also patiently listened to me as I have told him about all the others. It was Rick who suggested that I should find a way to share these tales with others so that they could learn to see and improve what they do using the seeing techniques reflected in the tales. So, Rick gave me a nudge (Gap Method at work) and the result --- What see is what we got.

I can see clearly now, the rain is gone,

I can see all obstacles in my way

Gone are the dark clouds that had me blind

It's gonna be a bright (bright), bright (bright)
Sun-Shiny day.

Songwriters: Kenny Gamble, Leon Huff